IN *love* WITH *me*

The 10 Steps to Self-Love and Relationship Success

Best-Selling Author,
Shannon Rios Paulsen, MS, LMFT

LifeThreads Books
Evergreen, Colorado

All proper names of persons mentioned in this book have been changed to protect their privacy.

Note: Due to Shannon's love of children and overall mission of peace, a total of 10% of the profits from this book will be shared equally with the I Love You Guys Foundation (In loving memory of Emily Keyes, their mission is to restore and protect the joy of youth through educational programs and positive actions.), Tuesday's Children (An organization that provides support and services for the children of 9/11 victims and others impacted by global terrorism.), and the Mattie J.T. Stepanek Foundation (Whose mission is to spread the word that *"Peace is for all people."*)

"Unanswered Questions" from *Journey Through Heartsongs* by Mattie J.T. Stepanek © 2002, reprinted with permission from Hyperion

"Let's Roll" (In loving memory of Todd Beamer, passengers of flight UA 93, and all other victims of terrorism.) and "I love you guys" (in loving memory of Emily Keyes and all other school shooting victims). May we always remember "Peace is possible" (in loving memory of Mattie J.T. Stepanek and all other leaders of peace in the world).

We bring their love and courage with us on this journey. May we all unite to create a more peace-filled and love-filled world.

dedication

To my parents: thank you for always wanting the best for me and for teaching me to believe I could do anything I set my mind to. I am grateful for our path together, so we may teach others.

To Jonas: my ultimate self-love teacher and partner.
Thank you for sharing this journey of love and peace with me.

To Emma Emaya: thank you for giving me the gift
of motherhood in this life. I love you dearly.

table of contents

Receive light.

Be light.

Travel light.

*You yourself, as much as anybody in the entire universe,
deserve your love and affection.*

~ Buddha

Introduction

Think about the fairytales you have heard about true love, all the love songs on the radio, and the many movies about falling in love. Now, take a moment and think about loving *you* that completely, unconditionally, and without fail. Think about looking in the mirror and saying to yourself those famous words from *Jerry McGuire*, "You complete me," and feeling a connection deep within. Imagine no more longing for the perfect partner. Really take the time to think about this for a few seconds. You are truly your forever partner.

When you love you, you have freedom to create your most loving, peaceful, and abundant life. It is who you are on the inside that creates your outer life. At the heart of who you are on the inside is how much you truly love yourself. It is only when you love yourself that a loving relationship with others will be possible.

For me, growing up in a turbulent environment, with chronic anger and fighting, I did not feel very safe, happy, or loved. As a teenager, I read all of the romance books that told me the prince was coming soon to rescue me. I was convinced this prince would solve all my problems and together we would create the perfect, peaceful, loving family.

However, what do you think I created in my life—after growing up in the family environment I had—when the prince finally came? That is right, a lot of conflict and pain.

It was devastating to me over the years to watch myself play out my parents' old patterns of hurt and anger. I will never forget how, on one awful night following a failed marriage engagement, I literally fell to my knees...and in that moment, came to some big conclusions.

First, the prince was *never* going to save me, I had to save myself.

Second, I had put a lot of blame on my fiancé for "not loving me." What became clear was I did not love myself.

Through research, discussions, and a lot of soul-searching, I eventually came to realize self-love was indeed the missing link to healthy relationships. Once I realized this, I knew from that point on I had to be fully responsible for my life and everything I created. I could no longer blame *anyone* else. I had to become healthy and strong on my own, so I could create lasting and loving relationships.

Could I really cultivate within myself this thing called self-love? Yes, but because I had limited role models growing up, it would take much work and many years of struggle and pain.

So, what have I learned that self-love is? It is a journey of falling in love with yourself and becoming happy with you, a journey where you do not seek to find happiness through others, but learn to access happiness from deep inside of yourself. It is a voyage of love, fortitude, and magic, but it can also be filled with anger, sadness, and pain. The road can be winding and long, and even scary, but the trip is worth every second because you deserve the happiness that falling in love with yourself brings.

My journey of self-love began many years ago with the first conscious memory I have of feeling unloved. It happened when I was four-years-old and it is still a very vivid memory....

I crouched down near the edge of the hallway at home and peeked around the corner slowly. I could not see them, but I could hear them screaming. The two people I loved and needed the most were arguing with such anger my entire body tensed. I was frozen in shock, barely breathing. I wanted them to stop screaming and hurting each other. Would they hurt me, too? Maybe I should hide.

I finally made my way back to my room and hid in the safest place, the closet, and began to cry. I wondered when this torment would end. The yelling reached a terrible crescendo and then stopped. The silence was deafening. Were they coming for me now? I was sure if I held really still they would forget I existed.

Why was I here? Why had I come into this family that did not love? Where was my safe haven from this storm? Why was it the two people I loved the most hated each other—and me—so much? Then, I heard footsteps… and sobbing. I held my breath and tried to be as still as possible, and then I realized it was my mom. She was crying. *She needs me*, I thought. I must come out, no matter what the risk. My dad could be behind her, though. Maybe they think I did something wrong. Maybe this is somehow all my fault.

When I looked up at her, I realized my mom was as traumatized as I felt. Through sobs, she said Dad was very mean to her. My childish mind processed this very fast. My dad did this; he is a monster. I saw a small trickle of blood run down her forehead. Now I really couldn't breathe. I had no idea what to do, so I told her it would be okay, I loved her, and would take care of her. My body was rigid, and I was barely breathing.

All of a sudden, Mom started throwing my clothes into a suitcase and said, "We are going to Grandma's. Your father is a bad man and we must get out of here now."

The tension rose in my body, but I started to feel excited. We were going to leave Dad, the big monster. We had a new plan to be safe—and even happy.

At this point, though, terror returned. What if he stopped us? What if he didn't allow us to leave and be happy?

Mom hurriedly picked me up to carry me out to the car. He didn't really seem to care we were leaving. He probably didn't love us anyway; at least that was what Mom said. Mom said something in anger to him. They sure knew how to be mean to each other. I put my head on her shoulder, so I didn't have to see him. Whew. We escaped, just past him. Now, it was my mom and me against him, the monster.

As we started the car, Mom realized she'd forgotten something. Shit (I probably should have been thinking shoot at this age, but I knew these bad words early on). Now, she had to go back in—right as we'd almost made our escape. As I sat in the car petrified, I wished Mom would come back, so we could get away. What if Dad was mean to her again? My breath again became shallow and my body tensed as I envisioned the worst. What if Mom didn't come back and I was left with him? What if I was left in this cold car all night? What if I died here?

After what seemed like an hour to me as a four-year-old, but was probably only ten minutes, Mom returned. To my horror and complete amazement, she said, "We're staying. Get your stuff; we are going back inside. Time for you to go to bed."

I was in shock as Mom carried me into the house. She tucked me into bed as if the whole horror movie had never taken place. I was not feeling a bit sleepy as I lay in bed that night with my whole body tense and scared. Terror, excitement, and sadness were all swirling around inside me. Clutching my beloved teddy bear, I cried myself to sleep.

At four-years-old, my patterns in life were set in full force. My body was taking on numerous stress and fear-based emotions. I was learning the cycle of fight and return. I was learning that people could be so vicious and mean to each other while still loving each other. I was learning the world was not a safe and loving place.

For me, some portion of this family pattern continued off and on until I was twenty-one when my parents eventually divorced. For many years, I still felt lonely and sad as I watched old patterns surfacing in my own relationships. I lived for a long time with the fear I could not have successful romantic relationships because I had no role models.

What I can tell you, though, is as I have become more at peace with myself, these fears have lessened significantly. This is a result of finding my inner love of me—and realizing this love can never come from anyone else.

I tell this story to allow you to have a glimpse into why my journey of self-love has been so important to me as an adult. I was not provided the understanding and foundation for loving myself as a child. You may have had a similar incident in your life or yours may have been worse. You also may not remember any specific incident, but you know—in your heart—that somehow loving yourself more deeply will provide the path to peace and happiness in your life.

Loving yourself is a process that can be hard to understand. Many people have told me they are really uncertain what this actually means. My explanation is it is a realization that you don't need anyone else to fill you and love you. You fully learn to love yourself, with or without a partner.

When you have deep self-love, you know you can take care of yourself and be your own best friend. You are your own best mother; you treat yourself with extreme care and loving-kindness. This allows you to create healthier and happier relationships in your life. There is no end goal for self-love; rather, it is a continuous journey to remember to live from your best self.

Each of you has the ability to love yourself fully and accept your deep and pure beauty. However, your beauty can be buried deep inside under a lot of junk. If you continue living from your old junk, you simply create new junk in your future. The lessons and the coaching I will provide you within this book will allow you to access and clear the junk so you can cultivate self-love.

Once I realized self-love was my key to successful relationships, I set out on a quest. I knew I would need to share my experience with others, so I documented the entire journey. I had no idea it would take twelve years to write this book, and I am glad I did not know this fact then. During these dozen years, I have become a life coach and a licensed therapist and have worked with thousands of clients. My goal in writing this book is to share with you everything I learned on my own path and from working with others. I did this so your journey to happiness may be easier. I can tell you I only want the best for you because I know in my heart you deserve it just as I did.

In this coaching guide and workbook, we will go through the ten steps essential to achieving self-love and, as your coach, I will be with you every step of the way. I have been a coach for hundreds of clients over the last thirteen years. I have also had my own coach the entire time. Coaching has been one of the biggest keys to my personal success. I am including priceless hours of what I learned in this one simple book. From the start, you should know you truly *already* have all the answers to your own healing and potential. Coaching will allow you to uncover these answers.

Coaching is a river that runs very deep and your transformation will be deep. As you work through the book, you will grow stronger and develop the strength to take the self-love high road laid out for you. It will lead to amazing things in this lifetime.

You have chosen this book because you have chosen love, life, peace, joy, connection, success, and happiness in this lifetime. Self-love will be the greatest gift you give yourself and the world. What I know for sure is the world needs you and your unique gifts. If you want the following things, self-love can provide them:

- You want to have **satisfying relationships** with your life partner and children.
- You want to **move closer to your purpose** in this lifetime.
- You want to **achieve a higher level of performance** in any area of life.
- You want to raise **healthy and happy children.**
- You want to achieve a greater level of **inner peace.**
- You want to contribute to **world peace.**
- You want world leaders to operate from a place of **love** rather than fear.
- You want a **healthy, available, loving partner in your life.**
- You want to experience **joy** each day.
- You want to look back on your life in the instant you know it is over and know you **contributed all you could** in this lifetime.

- You want to leave this Earth in a peaceful state, knowing your **work and love is complete**.

I will be your guide on this journey of self-love and will share a little of who I am as we go along. In the following chapters, I will continue to include a story or two from my own personal journey. These will help provide you with an understanding of my life and experiences as they relate to that chapter. I share them so you can know me, your writer and coach. As you learn to deeply love and accept yourself, it is crucial to share yourself and be vulnerable with others.

Getting the Most out of This Book

No matter what your current romantic relationship status is, this book holds the key to your ultimate success in *any* relationship. Each chapter contains both lessons and coaching actions for you to follow. The aim of each chapter is to guide you in taking action to move your life forward.

Moreover, I believe we must actually do the work versus just reading the book. I recommend you read the book chronologically and do the coaching actions if you want to receive ultimate value. However, you can, in times of need, open the book and turn to exactly what you need to hear in the present moment.

My goal is to allow you to understand and know at a deep level, you can always manifest the right experience, lesson, or resource that will allow you to experience self-love.

I have chosen to use the term Higher Power in this book. You will also find prayers and meditations. I have to admit, I believe in angels and their ultimate love and presence. I ask you to name your own Higher Power, whatever it is. I truly believe there is a Higher Power guiding each of you, whatever you choose to call it. This power will assist you and guide you if you ask it to. Your Higher Power is whatever you believe can assist you in being supported in a positive way during your journey of life and love.

However you decide to use this book, my only wish is it will impact you in ways you never dreamed or imagined, it will propel you to new levels of living and loving in the world, and it will allow you to leave your unique legacy here in the world.

While you are learning to love yourself, you must commit to spending even more time with yourself—loving, taking care of, and nurturing *you*. This is about falling in love with you. You are not here to focus on others. You must learn to cherish this time with yourself and know you deserve this time. You are truly the one who can love you best. The success of all other relationships is determined by one foundational relationship; the relationship you cultivate with yourself.

Thank You from My Heart

I want to deeply thank you for sharing this journey with me. The teachings come from my universal heart and soul as I was guided in my own personal healing. They are my gift to you. Remember, I am really here with you as you read this book. Always see and feel me supporting you and encouraging you. Honestly, you, my reader, were with *me* every step of the way as I wrote. Some days, knowing I was partnering with all of you was what allowed me to press forward.

This is the path less traveled. Each of you will benefit from this book in the way it will serve you and the world the best. I wish you infinite love, light, and peace.

Shannon Rios Paulsen, MS LMFT
www.healthychildrenofdivorce.com
www.inlovewithme.com
www.manifestingbaby.com
www.rioscoaching.com

COURAGEOUSLY CHOOSE TO LOVE
YOURSELF FIRST

Do you ever wonder why the United States has a divorce rate of fifty percent (it is on the rise in many other countries, as well)? Have you wondered why so many children live in physical and emotional poverty in one of the wealthiest countries in the world, the United States?

When you are not living from love, you are living from fear. When you live from a state of fear, you may create illness, depression, violence, high conflict, divorce, children who are not emotionally or physically nourished, and men and women who feel totally alone in the world. If you do not have peace and love inside of yourself, you cannot produce peace outside in the world.

Right now, when our world is so desperately hurting, is the time for all of us to do our part to heal the hurt. The single most important thing we can do is to heal ourselves through learning to love ourselves. Through the journey of falling in love with yourself, you can individually access the infinite power of love needed to heal our world collectively. If you have ever looked at the world and thought, "This is hopeless. What could I ever do to help?" You now have your answer. When you heal yourself and learn to love yourself, you will begin a path to healing the world.

Simply put, self-love is the greatest gift you can give yourself, your children, and the world.

This journey of self-love is a courageous one. It is courageous because we are not taught about this journey in school, and we probably did not learn a lot about it from our parents or from others in our life. No matter where you are now, a higher degree of self-love is attainable, and this book provides you with a roadmap.

Let's take a moment to get started right now to connect deeply with why self-love is so crucial for you in this lifetime. You will find your level of self-love equates directly to the success you will achieve in life. Self-love is the simplest formula to your ultimate success in life.

COACHING ACTION

Step 1: Take a few moments right now to take three deep breaths. In through your nose and out through your mouth, relaxing your body with each breath.

Step 2: Connect to the love inside you. Put your hand on your heart and imagine love there.

Step 3: Think about the top three things you could have in your life that would allow you to close your eyes at the end of this journey and say, *well done*. See them now in your imagination.

Step 4: Write them down below in the present tense format (e.g., I have three peace-filled loving children I am very connected to, my books touched millions, loving home/partner).

1. _____
2. _____
3. _____

Step 5: Feel the emotions of happiness and contentment you will experience when you look back on your life and see what you have created.

Step 6: Know in your heart, they are one-hundred percent probable if you commit to this self-love journey.

Step 7: Now, ask yourself one last question to determine if this book and the exercises contained within are for you. Do you believe taking eight to ten hours to read this book and do the exercises is worth the return on investment to bring these top three areas into your life? If the answer is yes, let's get started. What are you waiting for? You have your amazing life to create and live.

Choosing You—Lesson 1: You Hold the Key to Choose You

I want to be perfectly clear: You hold the blank canvas. This book will provide you with many ideas and colors of paints. However, *you* will choose what paints will work best for you in your life. None of us will follow the exact same path to self-love. You will learn from the wisdom and exercises in this book, so you can create your own masterpiece.

Our bodies and souls naturally want to heal and you will find the best healing path for you. You are simply brilliant, and once given the resources, you will know what steps to take in your life.

As a child, I did not feel chosen. I was always told my mom's life was difficult because I was conceived when she was seventeen. She told me she had no intention of getting pregnant with me, so I grew up believing I was a regrettable mistake. It took me many years to come to terms with this feeling of being unwanted, but as it turned out, it was exactly the impetus I needed to become the person I am today. It has shaped my life and allowed *me* to choose myself.

Today, after all the years of actually feeling unwanted in some ways, I look in the mirror and say, "I choose you."

You can choose *you*, too. You are the only one who can fully and completely love you. Loving you—all of you—allows you to manifest your love in the world and make a difference to everyone with whom you come in contact.

It is important for you to choose yourself. If you don't, you cannot allow anyone else to choose you, either. Choosing yourself opens a huge space for you to allow others to love you completely.

Unfortunately, so often, until you choose you, you never feel you are enough. We have many different "not enough" stories about parents, caregivers, or partners not choosing us or loving us, but whatever yours is, it is time to leave it in the past. The important first step is *you* make the choice to love yourself first.

COACHING ACTION

It is time, right now, to choose you. Look at yourself in a mirror and say to yourself three times, *I choose you. It does not matter at all what has happened in the past, I choose to love you. I choose to love you, and I choose to take care of you.*

Take a deep breath and let these statements really sink into your heart and mind. Know by choosing to love you, and accept you just as you are, you are opening yourself to a state of grace and beauty like none you have ever known. Choosing you opens your life to infinite possibility.

Choosing You—Lesson 2: Make Self-Love Your Foundation

Remember the puzzles you put together as a kid? Remember the hard cardboard underneath, and the frame all the pieces fit into allowing you to figure out the puzzle? The foundation of this puzzle called "life" is your ability to love yourself. Loving yourself is like the foundational cardboard frame of your puzzle. Once you have that, your life puzzle fits together in ways you did not know were possible.

Once you decide to make self-love your foundation, your life begins to shift in positive ways. If you are single, you will begin to make healthier relationship choices. If you are in a partnership, you will take care of yourself in order to be a better partner and create a better relationship. You may also realize your current relationship is not the relationship for you at this point in your life.

If you are a parent or hope to be a parent one day, you will learn to love yourself calmly, so you can love your children in a healthy, non-codependent manner. If you have your own business, you will learn you deserve success and you will be better able to attract what you want in your business. If you work for someone else, you will learn to take better take care of yourself, set healthy boundaries, and learn how to create greater personal success in your work.

It will take patience and time, but it will all unfold the way it is supposed to. If you focus on loving you, it will all work out. I know, because I took this road.

COACHING ACTION

I ask you to make a choice right now, to choose self-love as the foundation of your life. You deserve this more than you deserve anything else in the world.

Take a deep breath, close your eyes, and feel this inside as you say it. Say the following aloud now five times:

I deserve to love myself more than I deserve anything else in the world.

Choosing You—Lesson 3: Take Full Responsibility and Live in Choice

Some of us, due to past history, fall into the habit of surviving life. Each day we figure out the best way to survive. This becomes a habit and, unfortunately, even if you have a great life, you continue to play out the survival story. You may feel you are merely surviving day-to-day. Whatever situation you are currently in, you live like you don't have a choice.

We also sometimes make the choice to blame others and circumstances for how our life looks. You will not grow if you continue to do this. It is time to realize you created every single thing in your life. You must embrace this fact first if you are going to be able to make changes in your life. As adults, you have created it all, the good, the bad, and the ugly. Once you accept this, you will have the freedom to move forward and make different choices.

The positive news is you can choose to change at any time. Choice is a unique phenomenon each of us possesses every minute of every day. You may say, "I have no choice but to go to my job each day." I challenge you on this belief. The truth is it is a choice. You could choose not to pay your bills. You could also choose not do your laundry and not wear clean clothes. Hidden beneath everything we *think* we must do, there is always a choice. There is a deep freedom once you understand this. *If this did not make sense, please read this paragraph again. It is crucial to understand how much choice you really do have in your life.* You are now fully able to make all kinds of choices for your life. However, as a child, you may not have had choices because your parents told you what to do on a regular basis. You also may have been living in a very difficult situation where you really did not have a choice at the time. As I personally reflected on this concept, I realized as a child, I always wondered when I would make the next *wrong* choice and be punished by my father, who had inherited his father's explosive temper. With my mother, I felt I could never "get it right" or make the *right* choice.

As a result of my childhood experiences, as an adult, for many years I continued to live life as if I did not have a choice. I was also still afraid of the punishment I would receive if I made a wrong choice (which at this point was only me punishing myself). Some of you have most likely continued to live life as if you don't have complete choice. The truth is you do have a choice every moment. You have the choice to create your life the way you want it to be. Your past conditioning can make the belief that you have a choice challenging to accept. However, with the right resources, you can move beyond your past conditioning and make a choice each moment, a choice to live your best life *now.*

The following is a quote from one of my journal entries when I was finally learning I had a choice:

November 2005: *As I walked today in the rain and cold, I realized we get to enjoy whatever comes our way. No matter where you live or what you do, your attitude is what matters most. I am happy to be alive.*

There comes a time when you must make a choice to have a good life ***now***. Whatever it looks like, this is your life in this moment. If you do not feel you have an amazing life, make the choice to accept that you personally have the power to change it.

COACHING ACTION

Find a quiet place and take a moment to recite these words first to yourself and then aloud:

1. I choose to take full and complete responsibility for all things in my life.
2. I choose to accept my life exactly as it is in this moment.
3. I choose to make choices to create something else if I want.
4. I choose to let go of old fears.
5. I choose to let go of old, unhealthy patterns.
6. I choose to love myself unconditionally, so I can love others.
7. I choose the road less traveled.
8. I choose me.

Say the following out loud:

From this moment on, I let go of old stories about my life that do not serve me in this amazing life I am creating. I choose to see my world from a beautiful new perspective. I will approach each day from a calm place of love, peace, and acceptance. I now choose my amazing life.

SHARING MY STORY
Choosing to Marry Myself First

Solo travel after the end of a relationship became a pattern for me during my self-love journey. I would go and find myself again after a relationship ended. It was a perfect way to move on and enjoy life fully again. Traveling solo for me is very therapeutic. I've met so many amazing men and women and I've done things I wouldn't have if I had taken a tour or gone with friends. Usually, on these solo trips, I show up with no big plan in mind and "go with the wind," which often feels like the most freedom I have ever had in my life.

My visit to Guatemala, at age thirty-two, was my first solo trip. I had left my corporate job and was working on my own. I had decided to take almost four weeks to travel. During this particular trip to Guatemala, I was grieving the end of a recent relationship that was as close to abusive as I have ever experienced. The good news was as soon as I knew a line had been crossed, I made a decision in that moment that this person was not for me. Earlier in our relationship, I had asked my Higher Power to send me a sign if I should or should not stay with this man and, just days later, the prelude to abuse occurred. At this point, I was fearful of him, so ending the relationship took a bit of time. However, it was a healthy step for me.

During this trip, I was staying at a wonderful hostel in San Marcos, near Lake Atitlan, my favorite place in Guatemala. I was thoroughly enjoying myself and meeting a lot of interesting people. One evening as I was enjoying a Mayan sauna with a group of people from my hostel, I met Oliver, a man from Australia. There was an instant connection. It was like I had known him forever and he turned out to be a teacher for me.

The small town of San Marcos was having a community fair, and there was a Ferris wheel we decided to ride. We were stuck at the top for a while and I remember his friend yelling up to us.

"That is how gringos die."

Yes, that Ferris wheel was beyond old. I had yelled to the operator, *"mas dispacio"* or go slower. I had been afraid, but when you travel solo, the fear almost becomes exhilaration. You learn to enjoy the journey. That is part of the freedom and fun. For me, traveling solo was the most freedom I had ever had.

Oliver and I connected so easily and deeply. I did not want him to leave. When he invited me to travel with him, I said yes. We decided to travel to a beautiful waterfall with amazing pools called Semuc Champey. Oliver got sick before our trip was to begin, so I went ahead, riding in the back of an old truck the entire bumpy, dusty road to this magical place. I'd hoped Oliver would be able to join me. When he finally showed up, he was still very sick. Taking good care of him made me feel close and connected and I remember feeling like his long-term girlfriend. The connection was so deep for me.

We then decided to travel on to Livingston, near Honduras. Once we got there, however, things started to change.

We met an Australian woman Oliver connected with and he chose to spend the day and evening with her. That was my cue to leave. As I was departing our hostel the next morning to take the early boat out of town, I remember Oliver looking me in the eyes and saying, "I am sorry. You deserve to be treated better."

Yes, I did. Oliver taught me, once again, that loving myself was the most important aspect of my life at this point.

The return boat trip was over-packed and treacherous, and at the time, I was scared. I thought, "If I die now, my mom will never know what happened." I summoned all the courage I had and continued alone on my trek.

After the boat, I took a bus and then a chicken bus—yes, there were chickens—and then another boat all the way to Lake Atitlan. It was a feat to make all those connections in one day in Guatemala. Times like these allow you to realize your strength, which was a large part of my lesson on this first solo journey.

I had a few days left, so I focused on taking care of me and continued my healing. One night, I rented a nice room at a small hot spring near San Marcos. I was the only one there and as I gazed up at the twinkling stars, an idea came to me. I did a wonderful ceremony and vowed to love and respect myself for the rest of my life. I got married that evening in Guatemala and I was married to me.

This vow and accompanying ceremony proved to be a turning point in my life. I knew I was loved because I loved me. This was a comforting thought. I also bought myself a beautiful jade ring on that trip, which I wore as my wedding band. I recommend this initial marriage to anyone who is single, but also to anyone in a relationship. To love another, we must marry ourselves first. It is such a wonderful way to acknowledge our love for ourselves.

My self-love journey had just begun, but I was now looking forward to it with anticipation. I realized I had the power to make myself happy. I am forever grateful for all I learned about life and myself on that first solo journey.

Choosing You—Lesson 4: There Is No Wrong Choice So Don't Limit Yourself

There is no wrong choice in life. This perspective can provide you with so much freedom. As I journeyed solo in Guatemala, I realized this lesson. To that point in my life, I often became paralyzed when I had to make a choice because if I made the wrong choice as a child, there could be a big, scary consequence. This fear plagued me for many years—until that trip. During that first solo trip, there were many forks in the road, but they all led me to the exact right place. I finally realized making a different choice just produced a different outcome, not a wrong result. More importantly, I learned to trust myself and know there is no wrong choice.

Let go of your fear of making choices that are wrong. The only thing wrong is judging yourself if you *believe* you made an incorrect decision. Promise yourself you will not get bogged down in judgment. As I always say, "We do the best we can with the skills we have at the time." Decide on a path and remember you can always take a different one. As long as you are open to learning from what happens, you continue to move your life forward. It's also very important you don't limit yourself with your choices.

> *If you limit your choices to what seems possible or reasonable,*
> *you disconnect yourself from what you truly want, and all that's*
> *left is a compromise.*
>
> ~ Robert Fritz, author, composer, and filmmaker

There really is no limit to what you can do in this lifetime. Give yourself complete freedom to play, have fun, and be a beginner—more on that in a moment. It does not have to be right the first time, the second time, or even the third. It is important you do not get discouraged. It is a learning process. Stay in the process and you will be rewarded with love in all areas of your life.

COACHING ACTION

Read the following meditation to yourself or out loud as you give yourself the freedom to make choices along your journey.

> *Request to My Higher Power,*
> *Please be by my side during this time of evolution and transformation. Assist me in knowing all is happening for my future good and my future life purpose. Allow me to remember there is no wrong choice and I don't have to be perfect. I thank you for providing me with the people and tools to heal myself. I thank you for loving me through this time. Allow me to continue making the choice to move forward and love myself at a deeper level.*

Choosing You—Lesson 5: Have Courage to Love Yourself through Failure and Fear

As you begin to love yourself, it helps to remember that like a small child who takes one tiny step then falls on her bottom, we are all beginners every day. Give yourself permission to be a beginner. It is okay to take small steps and to fall backward if that happens. If you don't allow yourself to be a beginner and make mistakes, it actually can slow down your learning process. In many cases, mistakes help us learn faster. Give yourself permission to fail. Failure is movement.

Sometimes we think we have to do everything right. Because of this, your old fears will come up during this journey. You want these fears to surface, because only when they rise to the surface can you be fully aware and examine them. The fears will help you unravel the cocoon of "lovelessness" you have been living in. This old cocoon you have built feels secure and safe to your ego, which wants to protect you from any more hurt. Your ego will want you to stay in this safe cocoon of your old way of being. However, some discomfort is a necessary part of the process. In nature, a butterfly can actually end up being unable to fly if it does not struggle enough to release itself from the cocoon. This unraveling is an essential part of the caterpillar's life process. Without it, it cannot become a butterfly.

You need courage to embrace the process of becoming a beautiful butterfly.

COACHING ACTION

It is now time to begin breaking out of your old cocoon. It is time to limit yourself no longer. As I began writing this book, I knew I had to challenge myself to face my biggest fears. I would like to pose this same challenge to you. I invite you now to make the choice to face your two biggest fears. I am asking a lot, but I *know* you can do this. Also, you may have many excuses—please let them go. They are not relevant. Take a stand for your life.

Facing your biggest fears forces you to begin to access deep confidence inside. You have to talk yourself through this as you write your fears down, and then as you actually do these activities. They should be things you are very afraid of and don't feel like you want to do, but deep down you know that facing them will provide something for you.

Write your two biggest fears here:

1. _____

2. _____

Now, consider what one step you could take to move toward facing these fears. For me, it was asking my sister to go skydiving with me. She said yes and it was one of our best days together ever. It was scary, but so exhilarating at the same time. I even had a video made of it to record the event in my history. I made it so you also may be inspired to do more than you think you can. When you commit to and make the choice to face your fears, I guarantee something will begin to shift inside of you.

You may be wondering, "What is the true significance of this type of assignment?" Watch my skydive video and you will understand: www.inlovewithme.com/faceyourfear

My two biggest fears were skydiving and scuba diving. I was petrified to do them and I have now completed both. I am grateful I did. I learned so much about myself and also how to receive support from others. They are two experiences I will never forget.

I want to be clear that this assignment is actually one of the most important because with this choice you are signing up for self-love. When you take on a task your body/mind does not believe it can do, that action provides amazing proof of your own personal power. When you do something like this to confront and conquer your fears, your body realizes how powerful you are.

Your mind is what stops you from moving forward with your body; they work hand in hand. The phrase "mind over matter" is accurate. In my case, with skydiving, it literally became mind over matter when I jumped out of the plane.

I can do this were the only words I said to myself. I jumped and never looked back… you can, too.

Choosing You—Lesson 6: Warning: Evolution Ahead

Just a warning, your life may begin evolving at a fast pace as you commit to the actions in this book and begin to make changes in your life. This is good news, because if you are ready, the shifts will begin to occur. They may not look exactly like what you expect, but simply trust your Higher Power to work its magic.

COACHING ACTION

With any good program, there is an assessment that takes a pulse on where you begin and where you end up. With this, you can measure success. It gives you a baseline to see where you are starting from, shows you what may be areas of focus for you, and helps you decide where you want to direct your attention during this process.

Simple awareness is the first step to any true change. Answer the following questions to understand where you are right now.

Love Quiz
Scale of 1-10 (1 = strongly disagree; 10 = strongly agree)

I believe I can heal myself.	1 2 3 4 5 6 7 8 9 10
I feel love for myself.	1 2 3 4 5 6 7 8 9 10
I know I have a divine purpose in this lifetime.	1 2 3 4 5 6 7 8 9 10
My relationships are healthy.	1 2 3 4 5 6 7 8 9 10
I can access a feeling of peace within.	1 2 3 4 5 6 7 8 9 10

I feel supported in life.	1 2 3 4 5 6 7 8 9 10
I have a healthy level of self-love.	1 2 3 4 5 6 7 8 9 10
I have skills to be able to return to my inner peace.	1 2 3 4 5 6 7 8 9 10

*Note: There is a copy of this questionnaire in Appendix B you can take upon your completion of this book. **Note: You can also take a longer version of this assessment (The Love Questionnaire), online:* http://inlovewithme.com/?s=love+questionnaire

Summary

You always have choices to make in life. Once you decide to focus on loving yourself, you make a commitment to change the course of your life. I can promise you this is a choice you will never regret. Self-love allows you to create healthier and happier relationships. Relationships are the crux of your success in life.

However, always remember you must say *yes* to yourself before you can say *yes* to others. If you don't take time for yourself, you are like a boat drifting at sea. Choosing to create this foundation of self-love is the single most important thing you can do to create successful long-term relationships in your life.

FORGIVE, LET GO, AND CREATE SPACE IN YOUR LIFE

One of the foundational pieces to creating a healthy, fulfilling life based on self-love is learning to forgive again and again. Sometimes this will seem nearly impossible to do. Sometimes the hurt will seem too great. I still have not forgotten an event in my life involving my parents and wondered if I could ever forgive them.

SHARING MY STORY
Forgiving My Family

The year was 1987. As I walked down the stairs to the sanctuary of my bedroom in our old musty basement, I said something that amounted to smart talk in the eyes of my father. I think it was, "Oh, right," or "Whatever." I was a teenager; I had a right to be frustrated with my father. I went to my room and locked the door. Before I could lie down on my bed, I heard the rupture of my door as my father broke the lock and burst into my room.

"What did you say to me?" His anger was so great I had no idea what to do and there was no escape. Once again, my words were going to get me beaten. My father took off his belt and began to hit me on my bare legs. I started to scream, but it was in vain. My mother decided not to heed my cries of pain. No one was going to save me from this man. I checked out mentally; there was nothing I could do. I was paralyzed. The pain was so great I could not bear it. I was now sixteen-years-old, but still no match for an angry man. He hit me and hit me and then left me to cry alone. I felt completely helpless. I had to leave this horrible place. I did not belong to this family. I sobbed into my pillow, wondering why I deserved this torture.

I remember thinking if my parents did not care I was hurt, who would? What was love anyway? I remember a teacher asking me what happened and I told her I fell down the stairs. Family secrets were not to be told. I was a good girl and I had to keep my mouth shut. As my parents had always told me as a child, little girls should be seen and not heard.

It would take years to be able to forgive them, but I finally did. To live an amazing life, you must forgive both yourself and others. Forgiveness is an essential key to achieving your goals of freedom and happiness. In forgiving yourself and others, you release the past and you allow yourself the ability to move forward.

When you choose to forgive others, keep in mind you are not saying what they did was okay and you are not condoning their actions. You are simply saying you will no longer hold any anger or resentment toward those who have harmed you.

Forgiveness—Lesson 1: Choosing Not to Forgive

Why do people sometimes choose not to forgive? The curious thing is some people firmly believe if they choose not to forgive someone, they are actually hurting him or her. In some way, this makes the person not forgiving feel powerful. Yet, choosing to hold onto resentment in your heart and finding yourself unable to forgive is poisonous—to you.

A wise person once said, "Resentment is like taking your own poison and hoping for the other person to die." How true that is. All of your actions and everything you create will be impacted by the negative energy of anger and resentment you carry around.

The truth: You are only hurting yourself by holding onto this old energy.

Another reason people may choose not to forgive is because on a subconscious level they see letting go of their anger as *losing this person*. This can be the case in a romantic relationship you do not want to end or when the loss is someone who has passed away. In either situation, if you choose to remain angry or sad (i.e., you are not forgiving something), this keeps you connected to this person whom you feel should not have left you. It truly can be your last connection to them and you feel if you let it go, you will have lost them.

The truth: Holding onto a person, alive or deceased, only keeps you stuck in the past and unable to move forward in life in a healthy positive way.

If you choose not to forgive, you hurt yourself and everyone who loves you. There is deep pain and stress that manifests from living in a state of non-forgiveness. Deepak Chopra addresses stress in his book, *Ageless Body, Timeless Mind,* saying it can lead to depleted immune systems and poor health.

If you choose not to allow yourself to practice forgiveness, you trap yourself in a Purgatory here on Earth. If you hold onto old pain and anger against others, you will not become all you can be. You will block your ability to love yourself and others.

Forgiveness allows you access to a road you have blocked off literally in your mind, a road barricaded with a sign reading, "Do Not Enter." When you practice forgiveness, the roads of life are blasted wide open. Forgiveness allows you to choose the road of life, the road of healing, and the open road.

You reclaim your own personal power when you choose to forgive. Once you forgive, you will then have access to love. You will teach, live, give, heal, and breathe new and wondrous life into the world each day. Forgiveness heals the soul. It is a balm used to tend to old wounds, wounds that run deep into the well of your psyche and subconscious.

Forgiveness is a seed of life you desperately need to plant within yourself. It is a prerequisite to and part of the foundation for self-love. Your soul longs for you to plant it.

Forgiveness—Lesson 2: Forgive Yourself

Sometimes we are hardest on ourselves without even realizing it. Many times, we have things we have not forgiven ourselves for. Uncovering these things is paramount to your own self-love.

When you look back on your life, you know you have taken actions that were not always for your highest good or in the best interest of others. Sometimes, as you peel away the layers, you begin to realize you could have made different choices. You see things from a clearer perspective. You realize you made choices you would not choose to make now with the new knowledge you have gained. It is of divine importance to realize the choices you made at earlier times in life were the best ones you knew how to make at the time.

You did the best you could with the skills you had at the time.

Forgive yourself for not knowing any more than you knew then. With the resources and skills you had, you were unable to make any other choice at the time. Know you only did what you had the capacity to do at the time. You took the skills you had, and you acted with them. You did your best. You do not get to hold yourself responsible any longer. It is time to forgive yourself. Let it go.

COACHING ACTION

Step 1: Finish the sentences below (yes… do this two times):
I need to forgive myself for _____.
Take a deep breath.
I need to forgive myself for _____.
Take a deep breath.

Step 2: Stand in front of a mirror or envision a mirror in front of you. Take a deep breath. Say the following five times, while looking at yourself in the mirror (if available) and hugging yourself:

It's okay that all those things happened. I was doing my best. I love you, I love you, I love you.

Step 3: Close your eyes and see the word "forgiveness" in your mind. Continue to hug yourself, take a deep breath, and feel the feeling of forgiveness and love. See the word and energy of "forgiveness" encircling or wrapping around your entire body. Bring that forgiveness energy all around you. Feel it under you, in front of you, behind you, and above you. Keep circling it and feeling it. Allow your body to feel this forgiveness. Accept the forgiveness. Keep breathing deeply. Accept that you are forgiven. Say to yourself, *I am forgiven, I let go of the past.*

SHARING MY STORY
My Story of Self-Forgiveness

At the age of twenty, during my first summer away from the family which had always left me feeling so confused, sad, and angry, I met a wonderful man. This man, with an uplifting presence, was beautiful, kind, and loving. A woman I worked with called him Adonis, which was so true for many reasons I did not know at the time. We spent the summer playing and sailing on his father's fifty-two-foot yacht, *Magical.*

The name of the boat perfectly described that summer for me. I was in love for the first time. The connection I felt to him was unparalleled. He assisted me in healing some of the old hurt and pain because he was the first man ever to tell me he loved me. He mirrored my beauty to me. He also saw beauty in me I could not see.

However, upon our return back to our colleges in Wisconsin and Illinois, I found myself fearful and doubting our relationship. I wanted to pull away from him. I could not believe he really loved me.

Moreover, because my childhood was filled with conflict, anger, and confusing love, I was unable to love and open my heart to him. I didn't understand this at the time. We both relentlessly tried to

31

SHANNON RIOS PAULSEN, MS, LMFT

make the relationship work, but I was not yet ready to accept a relationship filled with deep love. I know now I could not deal with the closeness and love I felt with him; it made me feel scared and vulnerable. It was a sad cycle.

In my confusion, I pushed him away. We tried to make it work a few times. I always wanted him back after pushing him away. After one of our big break-ups, I completed a deep self-development course. During the course, I finally understood what I had let slip away. I grasped the truth, I had loved him, but had pushed him away because I didn't know how to accept or receive love. For me, loving someone was too scary and made me feel vulnerable. During the class, I knew I deeply wanted this man in my life. This who man that had given me so much.

The fears that had been running my life had nothing to do with him. I contacted him and pleaded with him to see me again, suggesting we meet at his friend's wedding in Wisconsin. However, he would not allow this meeting, and I was so crushed. The pain I felt as I realized I would never again be with this man whom had loved me so deeply and whom I had pushed away was almost more than I could bear.

That day was one of the worst days of my life. I finally saw the big picture, but it was too late and he had moved on. For years afterward, I continued to be angry with myself for not being able to love this wonderful man. How interesting that I would punish myself, just as I had been hurt as a child.

As I continued to be angry about not making this relationship work, I was not able to create any other healthy relationships. I was stuck in the past, longing for him in many of my future relationships. I could not move forward and truly create an amazing life. I also continued to struggle with allowing others to love me genuinely, which was the very sad part of this story.

Years later, I realized through my own self-love work, I had done the best I could with the skills I had at the time. I chose to forgive myself, which does not mean I did not still have some pain and sadness. However, when these old feelings arose, I didn't dwell on them. Instead, I took the time to love and nurture me.

Forgiveness—Lesson 3: Forgive Others

We all have people in our lives to forgive. Sometimes we may not even know who we still need to forgive. As we discussed earlier, sometimes you do not want to forgive others in your life for various reasons. If you are not forgiving someone or letting someone go, I ask you to reflect on why that might be. Because whatever your reason is, you are holding yourself and your life back.

Consider this, your soul chose this road, with these other people in your life, so you could be provided all the lessons you needed to learn in this lifetime. Some of us then go on to use these lessons to assist others.

My life lessons have become the foundation for what I do in my work. Having grown up in a home full of high conflict and divorce was the sole motivation behind my business, (healthychildrenofdivorce.com), and my first book, *The 7 Fatal Mistakes Divorced and Separated Parents Make: Strategies for Raising Healthy Children of Divorce and Conflict* (http://inlovewithme.com/books). I do not hold anger in my heart for those who have hurt me; I choose to forgive them and look at what I can do with all I have learned. No matter what we've each experienced in the past, forgiveness provides us with a blank slate. When we forgive others and ourselves, *and* we do something positive with what we have learned in life, our best life can emerge.

Forgiveness opens the door to all of this. Even if you think you have no one to forgive, I challenge you to look deeply. Usually, there are many more people than you realize. Even if you cannot possibly understand why someone did what they did or why you are not forgiving them, I ask you to let go and live by this quote:

Forgive them; they know not what they do.

~ Luke 23:34

In His final hour, He forgave. It is time for you, in this hour, to forgive, so you may live a beautiful life.

COACHING ACTION

For this action, you will need paper, a marker or crayon, and a red marker.

1. Get a few sheets of paper. On each paper draw a circle that fills the entire page.
2. Write one name of each person you need to forgive in each circle.
3. List those who have passed away when you were young. This can include people who died before you were born if their death negatively impacted others in your life.
4. If your parents divorced or separated at any point in your life, put that event on one circle. In this case, think about who you might need to forgive in this situation (this could be you if you held some story here about the divorce being your fault in any way). We know children are not to blame for divorce but, many times, they blame themselves.
5. One-by-one, silently get connected to each of these people or events. Take a deep breath and notice all the feelings you felt in each of these situations.
6. It is time to express your feelings in a safe environment. Take your dark markers, colors, or paints. Allow yourself to release any old anger, sadness, or other feelings onto each of the sheets of paper with your marker. Let all your anger/sadness out onto this safe paper.
7. Envision your body releasing these old emotions and fear. Let it go. It no longer serves you.
8. Now, in red at the top of each piece of paper write the following: "They know not what they do." Look at each

piece of paper and say the following: *I forgive you. I grant you forgiveness in this life. You played the perfect role to allow me to become who I am today. I thank you from my heart.*

Forgiveness—Lesson 4: Forgiveness Is Our Teacher

It is in your best interest to realize these challenging people and events have given you so much. Look at them in gratitude. Have compassion for them. Visualize your heart opening to them. Always remember you are safe; opening your heart is for you, not them.

With this action, you are releasing the negative thoughts and emotions around these people and events. You are melding them together into the golden threads of your fabric of life. The thoughts and emotions are still there, but now they are interwoven into your beautiful tapestry. They are now to be seen as threads that strengthen you to allow you to be the peaceful being you came here to be. We are all pure gold inside. We have to do the work to uncover it.

Your being wants to forgive. Your soul wants to forgive. Our bodies, minds, and souls want to heal. The human body is conditioned for healing. Healing is the human soul magically at work. All of the amazing blessings in life can be yours if you are open and consciously choose forgiveness of self and others.

COACHING ACTION

This meditation helps direct your focus and energy to work through the process of forgiveness of yourself or others.

Close your eyes in contemplation and love.

Dear Higher Power,
Thank you for this gift of forgiveness. May it allow me to go forth and prosper in your divine plan. I am thankful to you for this process and this ability I have as a human being to heal from the inside out, at a

deep, core level. Thank you for allowing me to open my heart to forgive others. With forgiveness, I have freedom to love and create in the world.

Forgiveness—Lesson 5: Forgive Caregivers

Some of our deepest issues can be linked to our caregivers—the people who were responsible for meeting our basic needs (not necessarily our biological parents). Many here on this Earth have wounds, conscious or unconscious, related to caregivers. These early relationships are probably the most crucial of our life. It is essential this relationship, no matter what happened, be healed to the degree it can be.

My experience and training have led me to believe that as developing fetuses, we are well aware of the feelings being internalized by our mothers and other caregivers. If our parents did not want us, we felt it. If our mother was depressed, upset, or fearful, we felt it. If our parents were fighting, we heard it.

Once we are born into this world, we long to see our beautiful reflection through the eyes of loving parents and caregivers. If our caregivers are angry, depressed, tired, unavailable, or sad themselves, this reflection does not show up in our mirror, and we have no true reflection of our amazing brilliance. This usually manifests in us as a feeling of not being wanted or not being good enough.

It becomes our journey to find this brilliance ourselves. If your parents were not able to mirror self-love to you for any reason, you need to cultivate self-love for yourself.

To be clear, the feeling of not being wanted some of us feel from our experience with our caregivers is not the ultimate truth. The truth is the divine universe wanted all of us here. One wise ten-year-old boy I worked with said, "Saying they, our parents, did not choose us doesn't make sense because they did, duh." The brilliance of kids.

However, there still may be some anger or hurt that you hold, which needs to be released for you to forgive your caregivers. True forgiveness of your caregivers provides a solid and healthy foundation for success in future relationships. Even if you believe you do not have anything to forgive your caregivers for, I still ask you to at least read through this exercise and see what shows up. It may even be they passed away too early in your life and you feel anger that they left you too early—you never know what could show up.

COACHING ACTION

This exercise is designed to identify and release any realized or unrealized anger or pain associated with caregivers. For some of you, releasing anger may sound scary, but it is important to release it out of your body. Anger can be stuck inside of us. When we hold it inside of us, we are literally trapped by the anger. You will be making space, so you can create healthier relationships because this caregiver anger lives at the root of all your relationships until you release it.

Step 1: Think of your primary caregiver or caregivers—alive or not. Take a few sheets of paper and write their name or names (on separate sheets).

Step 2: Take one caregiver at a time and complete the following process:
Imagine what you feel they did not provide to you. This could be the love they could not reflect on to you or the nurturing you missed, the mistakes they made. Possibly, they did not tell you they loved you, did not take time for you, did not remain in your life (by death or by choice), were too busy or left you for some reason. You may never have processed these emotions a child when you most likely did not have the ability to discuss, process, and release your sadness and anger.

Step 3: Imagine in your mind and body all the hurt, pain, and sadness they caused you. Feel this emotion and pain physically. Close your eyes and breathe into this.

Step 4:   Connect all of this pain to what you have endured as an adult in feeling alone or not being able to be fully successful in relationships and/or in life.

Step 5:   Feel this pain that lives in your body; you've absorbed it. It has been with you for a long time. It is time to release it.

Step 6:   Tape your sheet of paper on the wall or on the floor on top of a pillow. Now, look at the paper and speak to the caregiver(s). Speak their names, one at a time, as if they were physically present to hear. Visualize them right there in front of you. Tell them about the pain they caused you. Speak directly to them.

Step 7:   Look at their name on the paper and see them (they are represented by the paper) and let go physically or verbally of all of the anger, hurt and sadness. Scream, yell, pound ground or cry out all of the frustration you have held in your body. Do whatever feels necessary to allow this to release from your body forever. Let your emotion go. Allow them to rise up like a volcano. This is your time. You may also want to curl up and simply cry, that is okay, too. Stay in this process as long as necessary. Visualize this pain, anger, sadness, and emotion leaving your body. You no longer want to hold onto this. You can also simply talk to them, expressing your sadness and anger if this is easier. However, I encourage you to do some type of physical movement with the intention of letting go of this emotion and pain.

Step 8:   Do this until you feel tired and do not have the energy to be angry or sad any longer. Continue to let go until you have no more energy.

Step 9:   Take five deep breaths and come back to your center. Close your eyes and visualize releasing anything else you need to. Feel the old energy you no longer need draining from your body and cells.

Step 10: Take three more deep breaths. Be still now and find the divine love that exists within you.

Step 11: Now, take three more deep breaths:

- In the first breath, breathe in life—the universal life you have been given.
- In the next breath, breathe in love—the love that is your birthright, which you are now learning how to give to yourself.
- With the last breath, breathe in peace—the peace that will allow you to be a peaceful master of any challenge.

Forgiveness—Lesson 6: Have Empathy for Caregivers and Forgive Them for Not Loving Themselves

My journey of forgiving my father began when I was twenty-four years old. Through an exercise I completed, I realized my father was just as scared of me when I was a small child as I was of him. He was twenty-two-years-old when I was born, and he did not have the first idea of what to do with a small, screaming infant.

My father's life was less than perfect. His father was an alcoholic. Growing up in that environment, my father had no idea how to love himself. Furthermore, he didn't have the first thought on how to love me, his beautiful daughter. My mother's father, after a long battle with cancer, died two years prior to my birth. When I was born, my mother was only eighteen-years old. She was living in deep grief and trying to survive. Through no fault of their own, neither of my parents had any idea of how to love themselves.

Take a moment now to reflect on your parents' lives. Put yourself in their shoes for a moment. Were they capable of loving themselves? If not, how could they be expected to teach you self-love? Forgive them for not being in love with themselves; it will provide huge freedom for your life. They may have hurt you. If so, it was because they were hurting.

What matters now is your ability to love you, so you can love fully in the world. I see that my parents were my greatest teachers because, without them, I would not be where I am today. Thank you, Mom and Dad, for your guidance, mistakes, and love—the way you knew how to give it. I only hope my children will be forgiving of me.

Remember, love from your parents can arrive in many forms. You do not get to judge if it was right or wrong; you just get to accept it was love. I can hear someone saying, "But my parents did not love me. They hurt me too much." This is not about them; it is about you and your life. It is in your best interest to find something, even the smallest thing that happened during your life that showed they loved you. Take any small thing—maybe they put food on the table one evening—and allow your heart to soften to forgive them. Remember, "They know not what they do." You are strong. You are safe now. If they hurt you, they can never hurt you again. You choose if you allow them in your life. Open your heart and forgive them, so you can live fully.

COACHING ACTION

Completing this exercise will allow you to let go of something (related to your parents) on an energetic level. We are all deeply connected and this exercise will alter this connection in a healthy way.

1. Take a deep breath.
2. See your parents in your mind. Think of the dreams they had in life that maybe they were not able to fulfill. See them as small, hurting children; have empathy for them. Know your parents were scared and possibly did not love themselves. They could not love you in those painful moments. The next few words may be hard for some of you, but please say them even if they are hard to believe.
3. Take a deep breath, now say these words: *From my loving heart, I forgive you.* Envision your beautiful heart opening and say, *I love you just as you are. I am sorry for the pain you endured. I love you,* (Mom, Dad). Take a deep breath.

Forgiveness—Lesson 7: Live in the Freedom of Forgiveness

Forgiveness provides freedom for you to soar. I challenge you to make a habit of looking at who needs your forgiveness in your life on a regular basis. You will be amazed who shows up. Forgiveness is the easiest road to freedom. Take it.

Freedom provides wide open spaces. In completing the previous exercises, you have created space in your life. You want to fill that space with all of your positive intentions. You can create anything. It is your birthright to live to your full potential.

COACHING ACTION

Read through the list below and think about what you truly want in your life. Allow yourself to feel in your body the positive emotions you will feel when you have these things in your life.

- Your home. Breathe deeply into these feelings.
- Your family and relationships. Breathe deeply into these feelings.
- Your work and the lives you are impacting. Breathe deeply into these feelings.
- Now feel the gratitude you will feel for such a rich and full life.
- Breathe into this.

Summary

Welcome to forgiveness and the beginning of your new beautiful life. Forgiveness of others and ourselves is a gift. It allows us to access our love for ourselves. With this access, we have space to love others more deeply and create healthy relationships. Remember to continue to practice forgiveness with yourself and others.

CULTIVATE ACCEPTANCE AND COMPASSION
FOR YOURSELF AND OTHERS

Everyone wants to feel accepted. You may look for it from others, only to find you feel they are too annoying or too critical to give it to you. You may seek it from your children, but they have their own priorities. You may believe it comes from your Higher Power and wonder why your requests are not answered. Seeking approval from others will never lead to true acceptance. This search to feel valued may take the form of filling your life with material things; larger homes, more money, more degrees, nicer cars... and yet, you wonder why you do not feel happy. You search high and low. The one place you forget to look is inside yourself.

Giving acceptance to yourself will allow you to find true peace and love, the kind that is real and lasting and comes only from inside. Once you find it, no one can ever take it away. When you find it within, you will feel valued in the world. It happens when you give yourself full approval for who you are. Not until you have given yourself this gift will you be able to love others in your life, including your partner and/or children.

How many times have you been in a relationship and one of you did not feel accepted by the other? Relationships are deep mirrors that will show you a lot a lot about this phenomenon including:

1. If you feel someone is not accepting you, often it is *you* who is not fully giving this acceptance to yourself.

2. When you see the imperfections in others, they are mirrors to your own imperfections or your lack of self-acceptance.

For most people, this need for acceptance may find its roots all the way back to the attachment relationship with your primary caregiver. It is directly related to the attachment relationship you had with your parents and early caregivers. Attachment is about the love and care you feel or do not feel from your primary caregiver. If you feel accepted by them, you become a child who easily trusts. You feel safe and secure. The trust you have with your caregivers forms a solid foundation for you to attach securely to them. When you do that, you feel acceptance. Your caregivers provide this first mirror.

However, if you did not feel securely attached and safe with your parents/caregivers as a child, you can experience deep anxiety inside of yourself. This anxiety can manifest in many unhealthy ways when you are in adult relationships. You may find it challenging to attach to others in a healthy way. You may become an adult who acts out in various ways with your partners or others in your life.

In my own relationships, if I didn't feel someone loved and accepted me, I created problems. The little girl inside of me was still crying out for love from my parents. I would demand attention from my partners through negative behaviors. I had not learned to love and accept myself; instead, I was demanding they do this for me. Subconsciously, I wanted partners to give to me what I had not received as a child, which was an expectation my partner could not actually fulfill.

I know I used to put a lot of pressure on my partners due to my own insecurities, and low self-love. I believed I needed this person to take care of me and make me feel whole. It has been difficult for me as an adult to feel someone does indeed love me enough.

I know when I am unhappy, it is my job to make myself happy, not anyone else's. When I don't feel loved by someone else, I know the only thing I can do is love me. As I learned to give this love to myself, my relationships shifted and became healthier and happier. When you deeply realize this, it is very empowering. You have to do the self-love work to learn how to take care of yourself.

It is my hope you will recognize these types of patterns, or similar ones, in your own life. Awareness is the first step. Most importantly, remember not to judge yourself as you uncover these behaviors. Instead, use it as an opportunity to practice for they are part of who you are, and you are here to understand them and work through them. Once you recognize and are aware of the patterns, you will have the ability to make different choices. This provides you with a lot of power.

You are the only person who can give yourself this gift. It is cultivated from within. One way to cultivate your own garden is to be gentle with yourself.

Acceptance of Self—Lesson 1: Be Gentle With Yourself

One of the keys to transformation in your life is being gentle with yourself. When you are kind to yourself, you accept yourself in the moment. When you don't do this, you are often thinking negative thoughts about yourself or others. You are not acting with true acceptance and you close yourself off from pure potential and possibility. This negative way of thinking diminishes your spirit and reduces your success and satisfaction in your work and relationships.

When you are not taking care of yourself, you get worn down, which can manifest as illness, anxiety, or depression. To ensure you remain healthy, you must take time for yourself and focus on being good to yourself. When you create time to focus on yourself, you preserve your own energy. You then have the energy to be productive and loving in your life.

At this point in your journey, "be gentle," will become your mantra. If you do this for yourself, your best life will manifest. The space you are creating can now be filled with love. Think of how loving and kind you are with beautiful, small babies. This is how you must treat yourself during this time. Picture yourself as a small fragile baby and be *amazingly* kind-hearted with yourself. You deserve this nurturing.

COACHING ACTION

Make the choice to do one or more of these each day:

1. Take time to be with you:
   a. Focus on your breath and being present in the moment.
   b. Take solo time with yourself—do something you love.
   c. Stay in bed for a day (or a few hours), read, and simply nurture yourself.
2. Tell yourself loving thoughts—be kind and encouraging ("I am beautiful, loving."). Self-validate and acknowledge yourself for the good things you do each day. Make a habit of doing this when you wake-up and before you go to sleep.
3. Imagine yourself as a beautiful baby—picture the love you want to give to that baby.
4. Practice doing one kind thing for yourself every day.

Acceptance of Self—Lesson 2: Have Compassion for Your Inner Critic

The Critic, as I call it, is the voice in your head saying, *"You cannot do that. That is stupid. What are you thinking?"* and many other negative thoughts that constantly run through our minds. Some of us are masters at criticizing ourselves and thinking negative thoughts. If you are reading this book, you are probably one of your own biggest critics. You may have no need for others to tell you what you do wrong or what is wrong in your life—you already do that quite well. You probably hold high standards for yourself and those you love.

Your Critic believes if it stops you first by criticizing you or paralyzing you with negative thoughts, no one else will have the chance to hurt you because you won't move forward in life. Do you see how this phenomenon works to keep you small, especially once you are really ready to be alive in the world?

If you listen to your Critic, you will find it challenging to create the life of your dreams. It will take every opportunity to come up with a negative thought about your plans or criticize you for your life. When you are in deep emotional pain, you can be sure the Critic is controlling your life. It's time to make peace with your Critic because it's an old, wounded part of yourself, a relic from an earlier time.

If you were criticized or held to high standards as a child, you may do the same to yourself as an adult. You may also have seen your parents criticize themselves and each other, and you now model their behavior.

No matter what the reason is for your Critic, the most crucial aspect around the inner Critic is to acknowledge its presence. The Critic is hard at work when you tell yourself you are dumb, you compare yourself to others and feel you do not measure up, or you make negative comments to yourself about your life. All of these behaviors prevent your life from moving forward. It is absolutely crucial to recognize when your Critic is speaking to you and in control of your life.

The Critic blocks your natural flow in life. What is important is to have a process to deal with those old untrue thoughts when they come into your mind. The best Critic strategy I have found is the Soccer Strategy below.

COACHING ACTION

1. You are going to pretend you are the goalie on your soccer team.

2. Whenever a negative or critical thought arises, you are going to envision that the thought is a soccer ball trying to get into your net.

3. You are going to block the thoughts from reaching your net (which is you).

You may need to block again and again and again. Over time, this technique works and those old thoughts will quiet down. You train your brain that you are not going to allow these thoughts to dominate your life any longer. This is training for the mind, just like going to the gym is training for the body. It takes time and practice to develop this muscle.

COACHING ACTION

Step 1: Tell your Critic the following:
   a. I thank you for_____
   b. I can now take care of myself because _____
   c. You should not be afraid because _____
   d. If you get too loud I will _____

Step 2: Have a plan of action if you feel paralyzed by your inner Critic. Some ideas:

- Go for a walk
- Exercise
- Breathe deeply
- Talk to a supportive friend
- Journal/write about what is stopping you

Acceptance of Self—Lesson 3: Accepting the Critic When You Are up to Big Things in Life

When you decide to do big things in life, your inner Critic often comes out in full force. The Critic's fears can even stop you completely. I have learned the closer I get to my life's purpose, often when considering a huge step in my life or when I am closer to completing my goals, the louder my Critic can be.

When I got closer to publishing my first book on parenting and divorce, I started to feel a huge fear. It's frightening to make yourself vulnerable and put your life stories out there for all to read. The Critic is so afraid of being exposed in any way. The way I was able to trick my Critic into quieting down so I could move forward was **not** to make it about me. I thought about all the children I would let down if I did not get my parenting and divorce book out there.

Once I convinced the Critic this important endeavor was not about me, but about all the amazing kids I would serve, it calmed down. This technique works for me, and it has worked for many of my clients. As a follow-up, as I edit this book, I received a review from a parent in France regarding my parenting and divorce book. His comments about how his life has changed since reading my book moved me to tears. This is why we all must calm our Critic, so we can impact the world.

I can assure you, as you become aware of and communicate with your Critic, it will quiet down. You will learn to manage it each time you recognize it is at work. You will be able to take your life to new levels as you continue to acknowledge its presence and work with it. In any decision, consider what weight the Critic has. You will make a much better final decision if you acknowledge your Critic's presence and what its concerns are.

COACHING ACTION

If you are at a crucial big step in your life, are afraid, or are getting stuck, and believe it could be your Critic who has taken charge, complete the following steps:

1. Close your eyes. Take two deep breaths. Think about the next step you are considering in life. Now, think about

the lives of others you will be positively impacting with this step.

2. Visualize all those people in front of you. This is not about you, it is all about them.

3. Say to yourself, *This is about* _____ (insert whomever this is about, this could be the population you will be working with or helping, it could also be your own family).

4. See in your mind how their lives can change as a result of you taking this next step in your life.

5. Envision yourself taking this step; see the impact it has on others (their lives positively impacted). Get in touch with the emotion you feel when you see this in your mind; this is very important.

6. See them thanking you. Really take this in. They are so grateful you had the courage to take this step for them (this could be family or others in the world).

7. What step will you take to move your vision forward, what step will you take toward creating peace in this world?

Acceptance of Self—Lesson 4: Beware of Other Critics

When you are up to big things in life or you are making positive changes in your life, it may actually scare other people's Critics. You may have to deal with their Critics in order to achieve your own full potential and dreams. Always remember if anyone criticizes you along the way, it is all about them and has **nothing** to do with you and your dreams. As I was about to publish my first book, a well-known researcher on children and divorce, whom I had asked for a testimonial, criticized my book title. It initially really hurt, and then I realized she had never even written a book. I felt her own jealousy was at the core of her comment. Don't ever let anyone tell you that you can't do something through the comments their Critics make.

SHARING MY STORY
My Replacement's Inner Critic

When I decided to leave my corporate job thirteen years ago, my parents' Critics were really worried; they felt much more secure with the great steady income I was receiving. However, the most amazing "other person's Critic" comment came from the woman whom my employer hired to replace me in my corporate job.

While I was training her, she let me know her husband was an attorney. She asked me about my life and then said to me, "So, you are single and you are leaving this job to work on your own? Wow, I would never do that." She looked at me like I had two heads.

I admit her comment bothered me for a few minutes. Then I had my own conversation with my Critic, who was getting riled up, too. Of course, leaving that job felt like jumping off a cliff, but I was prepared and I knew I could do it. Here I am, thirteen years later and I'm still working on my own. I have never looked back, not once.

I am here to tell you that you can do anything you want and you do not have to listen to the fears of other people. You can never be sure of what other people's Critics' motives might be—whether it's jealousy, fear, or a desire for you not to succeed. I have heard other people's jealousy is just their unrealized potential you are mirroring to them. I love that idea. As you develop your self-love you will more easily know when someone else's Critic is speaking to you. The following coaching action will give you the tools to deal with other Critics.

COACHING ACTION

Here are two steps to take:

1. When you are up to big things and you hear the judgment of others, stop yourself and say *no* to their Critic, who is now harassing you. You will also need to let your own

Critic know you are not going to listen to this other person's jealousy or fears.

2. Imagine surrounding yourself with love. Imagine surrounding your mind with peace and calm. Remember their Critic has its own agenda. You have decided on your agenda and they cannot stop you. Do not allow any of their negativity to affect you.

Acceptance of Self—Lesson 5: Accept and Have Compassion for Others

We are judging machines. We don't fully accept others. If we cannot fully accept others, somewhere deep inside we don't fully accept ourselves. What gives us the right to judge others? Do you ever find yourself making fun of other people or criticizing others? I used to criticize regularly until I became aware I was doing it.

Through my own personal journey, I realized this unhealthy behavior was an attempt at ego self-enhancement. If I knocked someone else down, I felt elevated. However, deep down it did not make me feel good to hurt others. I also learned this judgment allows you to keep yourself separate from others. In this way, no one can ever hurt you because you have distanced yourself so you can feel safe and insulated. You cocoon yourself out of fear, limiting your ability to love.

The following is a conversation I had at one point with my Critic about why I criticize others:

Why do I criticize others?

Because they could hurt you. You need to keep yourself separate from others and not love them too much.

How can others hurt me?

They could leave you or physically hurt you. You must be kept safe. That is my job; I protect you.

Why do I need this?
You could die otherwise.

Why else do I criticize others?
To feel good about yourself.

Why do I need that?
Because inside I am really small, afraid, sad, and lonely.

What can I do to help you feel less sad and lonely?
Love me. Acknowledge me.

Okay. What else can I do?
Let others love me; critical comments and all. Let them know I am here, and then I will not feel so sad and lonely. Perhaps I will become happier once you love me, and I will not have to criticize.

All people are deserving of love and acceptance, no matter how different they are. Remember beauty is truly inherent in all of us if we take the time to see it. Practice noticing and appreciating others' beauty and soon you will begin to do it automatically. You will also begin to notice when you start judging others.

Something special happens when you accept and see the beauty in others; you also accept and see the beauty in yourself, and you become happier. Being able to mirror the beauty of others is an irreplaceable gift you can give. I had always wondered why people had gurus; I thought it was strange to hold someone in such high esteem. Then, one day while staying at an ashram in India, I was face-to-face with a guru.

After this experience, I knew why people held their guru in such high regard. What I heard when I looked into the guru's eyes was, "You are pure love." He had such an amazing ability to mirror to others their own love and beauty. I then understood that ability was what made him a guru in many people's eyes. It certainly was an unexpected and loving experience.

Can you imagine what we would create in this world if all precious children were actually fully and lovingly accepted this way by parents, extended family, brothers and sisters, teachers, and everyone else in their life? Each of us can probably remember those people in our lives who fully accepted us and acknowledged our beauty. They usually made us feel special and accepted. What a gift.

COACHING ACTION

Through this exercise, you will uncover the power of appreciating the beauty in others.

1. Pick a day, and throughout the entire day, focus on the beauty in others. When you see someone new, look and see this person's beauty. Envision yourself as a mirror for their deep beauty. Be aware of your reactions and the reactions of those around you.
2. On certain days in your calendar write, "The Beauty in Others Day" and continue this practice, particularly with spouses, children, and co-workers.

Acceptance of Self—Lesson 6: Have Compassion for Yourself and Others during Difficult Conversations

Sometimes in life, we have to do things that feel stressful to us. It can be challenging to stay in your heart center and have compassion with yourself when you are anticipating having challenging conversations with others.

If you are about to enter a situation where you know there has been a long history of conflict, stress, or difficulty in voicing your truth and feelings with others, it is important to take the following steps *prior* to this situation. This visualization exercise allows you to stay connected to your heart and feel safe and strong in your power no matter what you remember to do during the actual conversation.

COACHING ACTION

Heart Meditation

1. Close your eyes and take three deep breaths.
2. Envision your heart—your beautiful, bright, and loving heart. Thank it for being with you today.
3. Feel your loving heart energy pumping from your heart. Take this energy and visualize it moving out from your heart and surrounding your entire body. This loving heart energy is protecting you.
4. Make a conscious decision to stay in this beautiful heart space when you move into this conversation or interaction with the other person or persons.
5. Take three more deep breaths and before you begin the conversation, imagine the person(s) are in front of you, continuously envisioning love around you.
6. Begin the actual conversation.
7. If during the conversation or interaction you feel yourself moving away from this space and out of balance, take a break, if possible. You'll be able to move back into your heart space and then resume the conversation. If you can't take a break, take a deep breath and surround yourself and/or the other person with love.
8. In a long-term relationship, if you feel comfortable, ask the person you are communicating with to remind you to return to your heart space (in case you get thrown off).

SHARING MY STORY
Tough Conversation with My Dad

This heart meditation technique proved invaluable to me during an emotional conversation I needed to have with my dad. My dad had borrowed money from me that I truly did not have to give to him. After many months, he still owed me some of the money plus the interest, per our initial agreement. I needed the money back so I decided to speak with him in person, to address this difficult subject. As I pulled my car into the bumpy driveway of his farm, I could feel my stomach churning with each pothole I hit along the way. As I saw him sitting in his chair through the window, my breath became shallow. I could feel my stress and fear rising. I had been very afraid of this man as a child.

Before getting out of my car, I sat and practiced the heart meditation. Then, I walked into my father's home and sat down carefully at the old wooden kitchen table. As he challenged me defensively about the money he owed me, I stayed in my heart center. I was able to stay calm, but I don't consciously remember thinking about it. I rationally explained how I had figured out what he owed me, and he was able to be rational, as well. I left that day with the remainder of the money he owed me, including the interest, and my heart was strong and intact.

This peaceful outcome would not have been possible without me being in my heart center. I would have continued to create the old pattern of interaction where my heart would end up feeling ripped open and stomped on. My father showed up as a different man. He even listened to me for one of the first times in my adult life. I have realized over the years that my father's anger is due to his own fear and anxiety. When I was able to talk to him in this way, he was no longer afraid of me. It is inspiring how others seem to change when we do our work.

Acceptance of Self—Lesson 7: Use Acceptance to Unshield Your Heart

Some people protect or shield their hearts in various ways by being defensive, unkind, or angry. In some cases, that creates two people who react to each other in this way, going to war with each other, and creating pain, sadness, and lovelessness. Acting defensively or even violently can be reactive and normal behavior for people who carry deep pain and anger, especially if that's all a person knows.

It can be a tiring place to live if you or someone in your life is always ready to attack. Your life can become a game of war. Make a conscious choice to drop any type of weapons you are holding. Choose to let go of the old, reactive behaviors and move forward with intentional, aware, and confident actions and responses. When you consciously stay in your heart center, you learn to trust yourself, and you can create relationships with more love, joy, and peace.

COACHING ACTION

1. Physically place your hands in front of you and open them. Look into your hands. What is there? What weapons have you used to protect yourself in the past? What ways did you keep yourself safe? How did you emotionally or physically hurt or shut out others in your life?

2. See each weapon in your mind, then physically turn your hand over and drop your old weapons (this may actually be a weapon that represents the fear, anger, or other emotion). Let them go. See the weapons disintegrating. You no longer need any of these old weapons and strategies.

3. Turn your hands so your palms are facing up. Look for any other weapons you see. Ask, "Are there any other weapons I am holding?" Listen for anything you hear.

4. Repeat this process until you have released all of your weapons (hands up and then hands turned over, facing down, then let them go).

5. Now, say this affirmation: *I choose to release and give up my weapons, so I may freely love and be present for my greatest purpose in this lifetime.*

Acceptance of Self—Lesson 8: Open Your Heart

To accept others and yourself, your heart must be open. Opening your heart means feeling more, being more connected to others, and being more connected to yourself. Envision your beautiful heart opening, so it can be loved and accepted in the world. With your beautiful heart open, the world is yours. Your life purpose will be revealed, and you will be open to whatever your Higher Power has planned for you in this lifetime. You will see the world from a different perspective.

Your world will never be the same again with your heart open, which is what this journey is about—your heart access. What if everyone had access to this unconditional loving space for themselves and others?

Three things may occur when you decide to open your heart:

1. First, you may feel more vulnerable as your heart begins to open. Just allow that vulnerable feeling, breathe into it, and remember you are safe. With this expanded vulnerability and a deeper connection to yourself and your emotions, you may feel pain more easily. You may also feel more sensitive during this time. Be aware of this possibility and always remind yourself you are safe.

2. Second, as you focus on opening your heart, you also may be present to amazing things opening up in your life. Others who have open hearts will be drawn into your life. Breathe and accept these good things.

3. Third, others may feel threatened by this different you. As you transform your heart and life, others in your life can sense this change. Because they are used to the former you, they may react with fear, jealousy, or anger. Change can be scary for those who love you. Love them just as they are with acceptance and remember their reaction is truly not about you. Know you can never change

them and their fears; you can only focus on you. However-
er, as much as they may fear your change, over time it will
actually create change in them as they witness you living
fully with an open heart.

COACHING ACTION

Think back to one person you knew who accepted you completely when you were a child, such as a teacher, grandparent, aunt, or
parent. This person could also be someone in your life now who fully
accepts you.

1. Close your eyes and envision this person.
2. Feel the love you felt from them. Bring back that memory
   of receiving love. Hold that warmth in your body. Feel
   this unconditional love in your heart. This is acceptance.
   Deeply breathe into this feeling.
3. Visualize this person looking at you adoringly. Look
   deeply into their eyes. Breathe in this feeling of adoration
   and love from this person for one minute. Allow yourself
   to receive the love. Slowly and deeply breathe in this love.
4. Close your eyes and say to yourself, in a mirror if possible, *I am completely loved and accepted.* Take a deep breath and
   repeat these words to yourself for one minute.
5. Now say to yourself, *I am perfect just as I am.* Repeat this
   and breathe into this for one minute.
6. Now say to yourself, *I love you.* Repeat this and breathe
   this in for one minute. Take time to stay with this feeling.
   Savor it. Know, at any time, you can lovingly accept *you.*

Acceptance of Self—Lesson 9: Peacefully Accept All of You

In 2005, I made my annual solo journey to the mountains of
Colorado. The majestic and rugged mountains seem to hold me mys-

teriously in their loving arms. They did not ask for anything in return, just that I hear their messages.

That year, their message was *peaceful acceptance*. Peaceful acceptance does not necessarily refer to life circumstances; it is accepting who you are in your present state and body. It is important now to accept who you truly are.

We are all divine creations here on Earth. Let's look at what is important for you to accept about you.

COACHING ACTION

1. On a sheet of paper or on your computer, write/type all the beautiful things you accept and know are true about yourself, (e.g., I am a mother. I have a loving heart).
2. Write all the things you have wanted to be accepted for in your life and have not felt accepted for (e.g., being single, your body shape).
3. Write anything you have been avoiding accepting in your life (e.g., end of a relationship, career).
4. Open your arms and stand in front of a mirror or visualize yourself in front of you, if you are not in front of a mirror.
5. Say to yourself, *I peacefully accept you just the way you are. I accept that you are...* (Read off each of the items on your list from 1, 2, & 3 above).
6. Cross your arms over your chest and give yourself a huge hug. Say to yourself, *I truly, with all the love in my heart, accept you just as you are. You are beautiful and whole just as you are.*
7. Take three deep breaths. Breathe into this acceptance.

Summary

Self-love is all about compassion and acceptance. In the end, your self-love and self-acceptance are really all you have. Through all of life's challenges, you can always return to your safe place of love and acceptance of yourself.

No Greater Love

Life sometimes passes by,
And we wonder why.
Love is not expressed,
All we must do is remember to look inside.
This is where our heart lies,
Strong and true,
Waiting to Love You… Forever.

~ Shannon Rios

RECEIVE ABUNDANCE

As I navigated the journey of self-love while writing this book, I came to understand the true importance of *receiving*. In the context of this book, it means being able to accept things into your life that will allow you to grow and move your life forward. I found if I was not able to accept this divine phenomenon, I could not manifest what I needed in my life to be successful on this journey of self-love.

To love yourself, you must first heal yourself. To heal yourself—physically, emotionally, and mentally, *you first must be able to open yourself and your heart to be able to receive what the Universe wants to provide to you.* If you cannot allow healing in your life, you cannot achieve abundance and love in your life.

The universe only knows and wants to give you abundance, but you have to be open to it. The simple truth is the universe wants to give to you.

You are the only block to this process. You may block this process due to fear, old beliefs, and societal conditioning. The good news is you can actually learn how to open up to the gifts the Higher Power wants to give you.

Let's walk together on this journey of learning how to receive, so you can bring all you are meant to have in this lifetime into your life. You deserve this.

COACHING ACTION

Take time to evaluate for yourself how well you receive by taking the following questionnaire. It will give you an idea of where you are at in the mastery of this sometimes lost art.

The Receiving Questionnaire

Please read the following statements and honestly look at your relationship with receiving. This questionnaire will give you great information you can use in moving forward.

Circle the number that is the best answer for you. SCALE: 1= Strongly Disagree; 2= Disagree; 3= Neither Agree nor Disagree; 4= Agree; 5= Strongly Agree.

QUESTIONS	1 = strongly disagree; 5 = strongly agree
1. When someone gives me a compliment, I always accept it and say "thank you" with no other response.	1 2 3 4 5*
2. I feel I deserve to be loved by other people.	1 2 3 4 5*
3. I am a good giver, but not a good receiver.	1 2 3 4 5
4. When someone says something positive about me, I stop and allow myself to receive the compliment.	1 2 3 4 5*
5. Receiving is easy for me.	1 2 3 4 5*
6. Receiving is selfish.	1 2 3 4 5
7. I don't deserve to receive a lot (wealth, compliments, happiness).	1 2 3 4 5
8. I know how to receive from others.	1 2 3 4 5*

QUESTIONS	1 = strongly disagree; 5 = strongly agree
9. I know how to let others truly love me.	1 2 3 4 5*
10. I deserve true abundance in life.	1 2 3 4 5*
11. I consciously receive it when someone gives me a hug.	1 2 3 4 5*
12. Deep down, I do not feel worthy of receiving.	1 2 3 4 5
13. I believe when we receive, we give.	1 2 3 4 5*

Take a moment to reflect on your answers above. You will see an asterisk (*) next to the number five in some of the questions. If there is an asterisk, the closer you answer to (5) five indicates you are good at receiving. If there is no asterisk, the closer you answer to (1) one indicates you are good at receiving.

1. What were your lowest answers regarding your ability to receive?

2. Where do these beliefs come from?

3. Choose one of your low scores to focus on improving that area of your life as you read the rest of this book.

4. What one action will you take to improve your receiving ability? You may want to read the rest of this chapter before making this decision.

Receiving—Lesson 1: Through Giving You Receive and Through Receiving You Give

There is something magical about the giving and receiving process. As you open your heart, unexpected gifts will appear:

1. When you receive from others, you are giving to them.
2. When you give without attachment to the outcome, you receive.

Regarding number one above, if you have not learned you are fully worthy to accept love, you may unconsciously close yourself off from allowing in the love of others. Others want the opportunity to give you their love. You deny them this opportunity if you don't allow them to give their gifts to you.

The following true story is an example of someone not being able to allow love from others. As I was buying a stone necklace, the artist shared with me the following story.

A woman wanted to buy a beautiful healing necklace with precious stones, but decided she would not purchase it. She loved the necklace so much, she told her husband about it and he contacted the necklace seller. He knew his wife had difficulty accepting his gifts, so he asked the seller if he could return it if she did not accept it. He presented his wife with this gift of his heart and his wife would not take the necklace from him. Broken hearted, he went back to the jeweler. His wife had not been able to allow him to give his love to her.

Do you see yourself in this woman? Sometimes you may create a subconscious block to love in your life. You may reject love or find you are unable to recognize the love being given to you. At your core, you must learn to believe you are worthy of love.

The truth is you are only able to allow others to love you to the extent you can love yourself. As you deepen your love for yourself, you are able to accept more love from others. And as you learn to receive love from others, you actually deepen your love for yourself. It is a beautiful cycle once you get it started.

Regarding point number two above, when we give without attachment to the outcome, magic can happen. My story below illustrates this fascinating phenomenon.

SHARING MY STORY
Lesson from the Orphans

I knew at a young age that I wanted to work with children in orphanages. I now believe this desire was there to allow me to heal the child inside me. This was not anything I realized at the time, I simply followed my heart and volunteered with children.

The day I heard about going to the Ukraine to volunteer in orphanages, I knew it was meant to be. I remember sitting in church that day and absolutely knowing I would go on that trip.

During those two weeks with the orphans, I gained so much more than I ever could have imagined. We bought meat for the kids (meat was expensive, so they hardly ever ate it). When I served it to starving teenagers, I saw the hunger and deep gratitude in their eyes. This was a moment in time I will never forget as long as I live.

We were also able to buy new underwear and shirts for the younger kids. We told the children we were going to be giving them baths and we heard their screams of joy because it had been so long since they were clean. As I witnessed them so happy to be in the water and have clean clothes, I was filled with love and deep appreciation for them.

It came time for me to leave after two weeks together. I gave the kids very simple gifts. My heart melted as those angelic children gazed up at me in their infinite gratitude for something so modest.

As our bus drove away, the kids were waving, screaming, and running behind the bus. I sat alone in my seat on the bus with tears streaming down my face. I immediately knew I had been given ten times what I had given to them. I learned more about life and love in those two weeks than I probably had my entire life.

In our society, we think of receiving as getting something. In fact, true receiving is giving something.

The children were such open receptors of my love; they gave me the greatest gift I could ever imagine. They gave me the gift of feeling deep love. What they gave allowed me to have deeper access to my heart and provided me with the ability to live in my truth.

I am forever grateful to all the beautiful children who touched my heart at the orphanages all over the world—Alexandra (Bolivia), Jose (Mexico), Karla (Guatemala), Carlos (Peru), Liza (Ukraine), Kolya (Ukraine) and the countless other beautiful children that opened their hearts to me. Remember, when you can allow love in from others, the way the orphans fully opened up to me, you are actually giving them a gift. I ended up being the one to receive so much from the orphans.

See photos and a video of my orphanage trips at:
www.inlovewithme.com/bookpictures

COACHING ACTION

1. Where do you block receiving in your life? (i.e., what do you want that you do not currently have in your life?)
2. Why do you do this? Just answer quickly, don't think about it too much.
3. Say to yourself, *I deserve to receive* _____ (and say one of the things you would like to receive; you can do this for each area).
4. What is my fear about receiving _____?
5. What do I need to tell this fear?
6. What can I do to release this fear?
7. Envision in your mind what you want and feel how you will feel once you have it.

Receiving—Lesson 2: Opening Your Heart to Receive

Sometimes, after years of protecting your heart, you live your life very shut down. When you close off your heart, you limit your ability to receive. You must focus on reopening your heart. This will allow you to manifest abundance in your life. Living with an open heart provides joy and peace.

COACHING ACTION

The first step to receiving and giving is to open your heart.

1. Sit with a straight spine, your hands placed palms up in your lap.
2. Close your eyes and take three deep breaths.
3. Allow your shoulders to go back and your chest to puff out. Envision your beautiful heart opening wide. Breathe into your open heart.
4. Say aloud, *I receive all the Higher Power has to give me.* Take a deep breath and breathe this into your open heart.
5. Think of all the things you want to receive, all your dreams. Envision them in your mind now.
6. Say to yourself, *I receive* _____ (state everything you will receive). Breathe deep into your heart.
7. Say out loud: *Through receiving I give. Thank you. I am grateful.*

If you want to continue the meditation process further, access my Heart-Opening Meditation, a meditation from my guided-meditation CD, *Meditations for Abundance and Love Volume I: Deserving* (http://amzn.to/13CCMDG). This is my gift to you for purchasing this book. Access it at http://inlovewithme.com/heart-opening-meditation-free-gift. I have a second CD, *Meditations for Abundance and Love Volume II: Manifesting* (http://amzn.to/13CCVaa).

Receiving—Lesson 3: The Relationship of Receiving to Attachment, Surrender, and Manifesting

As an adult, when you feel a void or hole in your life, you may end up feeling needy for someone or something to fill that void.

You may believe you are lacking something in your life. You then usually end up seeking to fill that internal hole or sensation of lack with someone or something outside of yourself. You believe if you find this person or thing, you will finally be happy.

However, when you are seeking something from a place of lack, you are operating from a place of fear. From this place of lack, you simply cannot manifest true abundance. This is because feelings of lack and fear actually repel your ability to receive.

I have learned when I am too attached to something, it will never manifest. If you are too strongly attached to wanting something, it typically comes from an unhealthy place deep inside.

The problem is you may not realize you are attached to something out of a place of fear. The key is to heal this fear deep inside yourself so you can let go of the unhealthy attachments. This is the only path to manifest whatever it is you want in your life. You must heal yourself deep within through loving yourself.

Once you heal yourself, you will not want out of lack or fear. You trust at a deep level that it will happen if it is right for you. It then becomes far easier to receive and manifest. Your goal is to be able to receive from a place of trust, love, and peace instead of from a place of fear and lack. This is true abundance.

SHARING MY STORY
Attachment to Having a Family at My Dream Home

I learned this crucial lesson of attachment and surrender after I purchased my dream house in the mountains of Colorado. I was sure I was going to have a wonderful partner and children there to share the home with me. I became attached to the idea of finding a partner and having children. However, the more I tried, the more it did not manifest. When I look back, I can see I was too attached to this outcome. Once we are too attached, it is coming from our fear or lack. I see now I truly was operating from fear versus trust. Therefore, I did what I knew I had to do to take care of me. I rented out the house and moved down to the city to be closer to friends.

Only after I made that decision did I meet my husband. Three years later, I now live in that house in the mountains with my husband. We have put in our paperwork to adopt and we also hope to have a biological child, as well. I had to release the home, go take care of me, let my fears go that I was getting older, and *trust*.

When I learned to surrender and trust myself at the age of thirty-nine, I no longer had to be a mother, a partner, or anything else society—and especially my family—defined as successful. I now had the space to design my own success in the world. I could let go of anything that was not bringing me peace in my life.

Once I did that, I could now be who I was born to be. This place of surrender and trust is not giving up; it actually allows the divine plan for you to unfold. When you are not clinging to old ideas that no longer serve you, you can manifest what you are here to bring into the world. It works best when you peacefully "allow." ***The only things that do not bring us peace are those things we are forcing for reasons other than what is truly right for us at the time.***

I clearly remember the night I met my husband—it was a few short weeks after I made the decision to rent out my house and move to the city. I had let go of all the old fear. I was living in surrender and trust. I was traveling solo in Thailand at the time and had done my own healing work alone in my cabana that evening, deepening my own self-love. I was walking to a restaurant and saw a happy couple ahead of me, holding hands. I remember the sensation of feeling deep trust rather than a feeling of want or lack. I silently said to myself as I walked behind the couple, "I am so happy I will have that one day." I believed it in my heart. That same exact night, there sat my future husband at the table directly across from me.

When we give love to and trust ourselves, we receive love.

COACHING ACTION

When you are able to show love to yourself, you begin a journey that results in receiving love. This exercise will help you do your own healing work to deepen your own self-love, moving you toward surrender and a deep trust.

1. Take a deep breath. Think of something you have been attached to having in your life, but you have not been manifesting in your life (e.g., partner, child, more money).

2. Say to yourself, *I fully release having _____ in my life.* Take a deep breath. *I release all worry and anxiety about this situation. I release any feelings of fear or lack connected to this situation. I completely let go. I am safe, secure, and beautiful just as I am.* Breathe deeply into this.

3. Say to yourself, *I trust that my Higher Power knows what is right for me with this situation and is bringing _____ or more into my life at the exact perfect time. I trust at a deep level it will happen. I choose to live life fully in peace and love. I will focus my energy on other things that make me happy. I am grateful for my life as it is right now.*

4. The key is to believe and trust you are taken care of. This outcome or something better will happen when it is right for you. Let go of *any* fear associated with this situation.

Receiving—Lesson 4: Understanding that Love = Money

You must believe you are *worth* it. Get it—worth it, to receive money in your life. If you do not feel you are worth it, money will never manifest and you will never have enough of it. In my experience, anyone who never has enough money can trace it back to a sense of feeling undeserving of having money. These feelings stem from a place of scarcity, which is actually a scarcity of self-love. This is the wonderful news for you; money is directly related to the ability to love yourself.

Another way this scarcity manifests is you may be giving to others, but if you are doing so at the *expense* of yourself and find you are unable to pay your own bills, you are dealing with self-worth issue; not feeling you are worthy of having enough for you. You believe you must give money away to feel like you are enough.

The other money phenomenon related to love shows up when we are afraid to share or give away any of our money. In this case, we also may be stingy with our love. We must believe we will have enough and be able to share our money in a healthy way with others. When we do this, we are opening our hearts to love.

Being afraid we will never have enough money keeps us stuck in survival mode in life. We live in a constant fear we won't have enough. Money brings up our most primal fears. Some of you may be afraid you may die without money.

SHARING MY STORY
Fear of Not Having Money and My Childhood

As a child, I saw my parents always struggling with money and I worried about how we would pay our bills. This created a deep fear inside of me of not being able to survive if we did not have money. As an adult, I went through a period in life where I had much more money going out than coming in. I gained amazing insight through this time. I honestly thought I was going to die without enough money. When I did not, I learned not having money does not kill you. There was a lot of freedom from old fears in this realization.

I have since discovered once I learned to give myself love, I would automatically bring in more money. When you love yourself, you will trust yourself to make money and you will have enough. Because you understand *you* are enough. You will also not give to others at the expense of yourself. When you manifest more than you need, you will also be able to share with others. You will no longer operate from lack or fear—your own or anyone else's.

The key here is to realize money is not what is important. What is important is to focus on manifesting and receiving love in your heart. Because if you truly operate from a place of love and give to yourself, you will manifest all the funds you need to follow your path. I have seen this phenomenon again and again in my life. When my husband and I made the commitment to adopt, it was simply amazing how the money easily and effortlessly showed up.

Begin to see money as love. When you write a check, see your love flowing into the world. Then see even more money returning to you. When you give love, you receive love.

COACHING ACTION

Take a few moments to go through these steps in order to focus on truly loving and giving to yourself. Find a quiet place and ask yourself these questions:

1. *Why do I, (insert your name here), deserve to receive money in my life?* Then, answer by writing: *I, (insert your name), deserve to receive money in my life because…* Write this question out and complete this statement seven times (example below):

    Why do I, Shannon, deserve to receive money in my life? (just one time)
    I, Shannon, deserve to receive money in my life because I will do good things with it.
    I, Shannon, deserve to receive money in my life because I deserve a magical life.

Answer the question above seven times with a different answer each time. *Trust* the process. Don't overthink your answers.

2. *Why do I, (insert your name here), deserve to receive love in my life?* Write out and answer this question *I, Shannon, deserve to receive love in my life because I am worthy of love...* seven times (with different answers) just as in the above example.

3. Once you are done with step 1 and 2, take a deep breath, close your eyes, and deeply breathe into these truths. Do this for five deep breaths.

4. Visualize your beautiful gold heart. Touch your heart, see the beautiful gold color. What does your heart want you to know about money? Ask your heart now, *Dear heart, what should I know about money?* Listen for the answer.

5. Deeply trust and believe you are receiving all the money and love you need to live your perfect life. Say the following: *I deeply trust and believe I am receiving all the money and love I need to live my perfect life. I am thankful.*

6. Close your eyes, take two deep breaths, and visualize all the money you need coming to you. See it in the form of checks, payments, and cash. Now, envision it going back into the world, creating love, peace, and change for others. Feel it all multiplying and returning back to you. Do this again and again. This is the true cycle of life and love.

Receiving—Lesson 5: In-Joy Life

Receiving and living from joy is a healthy place from which to live and create your life. How often do you truly choose to live there? Sometimes life does not feel very joyful. This is the truth. However, you can choose to receive joy and live from joy at any point.

I have found one of the keys to self-love is the ability to change your perspective. The perspective of joy gives you a strong foundation for your life. As humans, many times our first reaction is fear, and in fear, there is no joy. You must consciously choose to receive and live in joy.

The good news is you have the ability to shift your perspective through shifting your thoughts.

COACHING ACTION

This is a simple practice you can use to shift yourself at any moment to the place of joy, especially at stressful moments.

1. Close your eyes, take three deep breaths in through your nose, and out through your mouth. Allow your body to relax. Let go of any stress you are holding in your body. Take one more very long breath out, and as you do this, envision all the stress physically leaving your body.
2. Now, take the corners of your mouth and raise them up toward the sky. Yes, a smile. Take another deep breath. Close your eyes, if you feel safe doing this.
3. Now, it is time to balance your brain with joy. Close your eyes and move them all the way to the left and say to the left side of your brain. *I am pure joy.* Now, move your eyes all the way to the right and say to yourself, *I am pure joy.* Keep breathing deeply. Do this ten times on each side or get lost in doing it and don't keep count.

You can choose joy at any point in your journey simply by completing the above exercise. I encourage you to practice this at least five times a day and see what a difference it makes.

Receiving—Lesson 6: Focus on Receiving Love

The goal now is to focus on loving you and loving others. Love truly is all around you. The only requirement to receive it is for you to be open to it. It has been said by a very wise person that the Universe only knows abundance. Abundance means love. When you are open to it, you manifest it within you. When you sit in stillness, and look deep within, you will be present to this love. This deep love brings you to that calm place within. This is true peace.

COACHING ACTION

1. In a quiet place, settle yourself into a calm state. Lay your hands palms up on your lap. Say these words to yourself or aloud: *Higher Power, I am open to whatever plan you have for me. I release all attachment to anything that is not in my highest good. I surrender to universal love and guidance. I intend that today I will keep my arms open to whatever the world has to show me or bring across my path. I am of divine love and light. I am here for a purpose. I open my arms and heart to the world. Namaste.*

2. To begin the process of receiving, sit for a moment, close your eyes, and take a deep breath. Focus on just breathing and receiving the air. It is a precious gift. Feel this beautiful gift with each inhale. Breathe it in, and allow yourself to realize deeply that you are here to receive. Say to yourself, *I am here to receive.* Now, consciously receive the air you are breathing. Do this for your next five breaths.

3. Open your arms wide and stretch your heart big. Be sincerely grateful for the beautiful air we are privileged to breathe. Smile and know you are on the path to loving yourself. Breathe into this.

4. Ask yourself, *what do I need to receive to bring my life to the next level of my potential?* Listen for the answer. Know you are receiving everything you need and gently accept this truth.

Summary

Remember, to truly love yourself, you *must* learn to receive and give unconditionally. Otherwise, you will reject every good thing that comes your way. You will not be able to notice all the good in your life. As you receive, you let love in.

Through receiving, you will allow your life to become the cornucopia of wealth and love it is meant to be. This journey of self-love will bear more fruit than you can even imagine right now.

EMBRACE RELATIONSHIPS AS YOUR
GREATEST SELF-LOVE TEACHER

Relationships provide us with crucial information about where we are in our self-love journey. They are the foundation of our deep healing and growth for two main reasons:

1. The love you receive from others assists in your own healing and growth.
2. What happens in your relationships provides priceless clues to what you still need to focus on in your own healing and growth.

The truth is relationships are healing and provide you with gifts if you are willing to see them that way. Whether you are currently in a relationship or you are hoping to be in one in the future, you can assess your current and past relationship patterns and themes in order to bring yourself to the next level of relationship health.

It is great news you can use data from your past relationships to understand your relationship patterns. Once you understand your patterns, you can use this information to allow yourself to be as healthy as possible in your current or future relationships. This knowledge will allow you to grow to your next level of potential in your relationships.

COACHING ACTION

To begin to understand your relationship patterns, ask yourself the following questions:

1. Am I attracted to people who are unavailable or unable to show their love for me?
2. Do I hold anger or resentment toward someone in my life? Do I hold anger toward my primary caregivers?
3. Do I feel I am in a relationship that is not right for me?
4. When someone is able to show his or her love for me in a relationship, am I attracted to that person or do I push them away, or find fault with them?
5. Have I recently ended a relationship and not asked myself how to ensure my next choice is a healthy one?
6. Am I currently in a relationship in which I do not treat my current partner with healthy love?
7. Am I currently in a relationship in which my partner does not treat me with healthy love?
8. Do I blame the other person for the ending of any of my past relationships?

Your answers to the above questions provide information about where you can spend time loving yourself more deeply. It is important to spend time looking at your relationship patterns, which we will do in this chapter. When you are able to have insight into your relationships, you spend less time being frustrated or feeling like a failure. You will spend time creating happy, healthy relationships.

Relationships Heal Us—Lesson 1: The Impact of Our Parental Relationships on Our Adult Relationships

Perhaps the most important relationship you can learn about yourself from is the relationship with your parents or caregivers. This is the bond on which you base your sense of self. Taking time to reflect first on this relationship is crucial. Your adult relationship patterns are usually unconsciously linked to your first relationships with your parents/caregivers.

COACHING ACTION

Take time now to reflect on your parental relationships and how they could be linked to your current relationships. Start by giving some thought to the following questions (from my first book, *The 7 Fatal Mistakes Divorced and Separated Parents Make: Strategies for Raising Healthy Children of Divorce and Conflict*). Writing down your answers will be the best way to process these patterns.

1. What did you want from your parents/caregivers that they did not give to you (e.g., time, love, acceptance)?
2. How do you feel or know you were hurt by your parents/caregivers (if you were)?
3. What did/do you want from your partner or this relationship that they were never able to give you?
4. How can you relate what your parents/caregivers did not give you to what you feel your most recent relationship does not give you?
5. How is your past or current relationship similar to your parents' relationship?
6. How is your partner similar to either of your parents?
7. What did you two create together that was/is not healthy?
8. Why did you choose this person (usually subconsciously)?
9. If your past or current relationship partner did something terrible to you, how might this be a link to other pain you may have suffered in your life (such as abuse or neglect)?
10. Have you seen this pattern played out in any of your other relationships?

11. What story do you tell yourself? (e.g., I don't deserve a kind partner, all partners leave, men/women are bad).
12. When you look at the relationship, did/do you push away healthy love (that they may have given to you)?
13. What old hurts do you see in yourself that you may have been trying to heal by choosing this person?
14. Now, for the following questions, take a deep breath and ask yourself (and quietly listen for the answer):
15. What patterns of my parents or caregivers am I playing out?
16. What do I need to give myself instead of seeking it from others?
17. What do I need to do to heal this hurt?
18. What different choices do I want to make in my relationships?
19. What is the gift this person gave or is giving to me?
20. What gifts/lessons about self-love did your parents provide for you (usually as challenges) that you are now learning or need to learn in your current or future relationships?

Take a moment now and silently thank your past or current partner from your heart for the lessons they taught you, and truly honor the learning from this relationship.

Relationships Heal Us—Lesson 2: Relationships as Mirrors

When I was engaged at age twenty-nine, I told my fiancé, "I just want you to love me. You are not loving me." Once the relationship ended, I was brought to my knees from the pain and I reflected deeply on what had happened.

I finally realized something important—I did not love myself. I was telling him I wanted him to love me, but I was not truly able to love myself. I also realized I was not good at accepting his love when he did give it to me. I could not take in his love.

In reflecting back on this relationship and other unsuccessful relationships, I realized I had to be accountable. I finally realized I was the common denominator in my failed relationships. I could no longer blindly blame other people. I could finally see the huge role I had played in my unsuccessful relationships.

Amazingly, we tend to attract into our lives scenarios that provide healing opportunities for us romantically, professionally, and personally. It is important to look at any patterns you see showing up at home and/or work. Is someone always disappointing you? Is someone always being mean to you? What other patterns have you noticed, particularly those patterns of not being satisfied in relationships? Relationships are always some type of mirror—they reflect what is going on inside of you. What you notice and experience in your relationships with others usually results from some belief inside of you. For example, if you allow someone to continue to hurt you, somewhere deep inside you believe you deserve to be hurt. These old beliefs are important to uncover. Once you uncover them and focus on giving yourself whatever you have wanted, but are not receiving from others, your life can completely shift.

COACHING ACTION

The first step in recognizing relationship patterns is to reflect back on what you felt the other person did not give you or what you felt they did wrong. This will give you information about yourself.

1. Choose an issue that frustrated you in a past relationship or partnership. This issue should be about the relationship or person, what you feel they did not provide you, or what frustrating experience you had with them. Whatever the issue was, I can guarantee you it is a mirror for you in some way that reflects something inside of you.

2. Think about what this issue could be reflecting off you in your life. If this person was unkind to you, are you also unkind to yourself? Reflect on this issue to see what it is mirroring to you. What is this frustration telling you about yourself? Is it there for you to learn from it?

3. What do you need to give to yourself? Complete this sentence:

I am frustrated that (A = name of person) did not/does not provide (B = whatever you want from them) to me. However, the truth is: I am frustrated I don't provide (whatever you said above in B) to me.

4. What steps can you take to give yourself what you need (B above)?

The key is to stop expecting everything you need to come from others.
***You** must first meet your own needs.*

Relationships Heal Us—Lesson 3: The Unconditional Love of Others

The love of others assists you in your own healing. No matter what the outcome of a relationship is, even if it ended and you did not want it to, if you take the time to reflect, you will see the other person assisted you in loving yourself at a deeper level.

When a good and loving man unconditionally loved me for the first time, I saw my own beauty. Growing up in the home environment I experienced as a child, I was not able to see my full beauty. The love he gave me reflected that beauty and I was finally able to see it on some level. This man also gave me the gift of trust, and because I trusted him, I learned to better trust myself. These gifts from him were priceless. Even though I was unable to stay with him and accept this unconditional love, he was one of my greatest teachers and healers. I am grateful to him. Below is a quote from a card I gave to him the first summer we met. At the time, I had no idea of the deep significance of the words or what he had given me.

Reflections of the times we've shared mirror some of my fondest memories.

COACHING ACTION

1. Reflecting back on your past relationships, what positive things did they mirror to you?
2. What beautiful things did you see about yourself through relationships?
3. What gifts did your past relationships give you?

Relationships Heal Us—Lesson 4: When We End an Unhealthy Relationship

If you make the choice to end a relationship where someone does not love you in a healthy way, this is healing. In this case, you have taken a stand to love yourself. No matter what happened in the relationship, once you recognize and stand up to unhealthy behavior, you have ended that old pattern. You are no longer attracted to this type of behavior. You have set a clear boundary.

Whatever it was you stood up to—drugs, drinking, yelling, anger, or disrespect—you will not attract that level of unhealthiness again. This is because you have moved to a new level of health.

In my situation, I consciously said no to alcoholics, mental illness, and continuous anger before meeting my husband. He is none of those things. I believe when we consciously say "no," we have healed that old part of ourselves and will no longer attract that into our lives. Now, this is some good news.

SHARING MY STORY
Saying No to an Unhealthy Relationship

When I was living alone in my home in the mountains and longing for a partner, I met a man who was also a counselor who lived in my same town. There was an attraction and we had a couple of dates. On our third date, he showed up at my house after working and being at the gym, smelling of alcohol. When I asked him about it, he shared that he had struggled with addiction in his past and obviously was struggling again. I told him I could no longer date him. His question to me was, "Haven't I treated you well?" My response was, "You have treated me fine, but you are not treating yourself well enough right now." Standing up for myself and him was a defining moment for me and my dating career.

COACHING ACTION

1. When in the past have you said no to something unhealthy in your relationship?
2. Can you see you have healed that aspect and are attracting healthier people in that area now?
3. Is there anything in your current relationship you need to say no to? If you are not in a relationship, take some time to reflect on your past relationships. Is there anything you need to be sure to say no to in your next relationship?

Relationship Themes

These themes are different ways we respond in a relationship that usually do not allow us to create healthy partnerships. Unfortunately, sometimes these patterns can be hard to see because they have become such a habit. Your old anxieties and fears can cause you to operate from an old, untrue, subconscious story you are telling yourself. These old stories form our relationship themes.

This chapter helps you identify them. Once you identify your themes and understand how you can change your behavior related to them, you will be able to create healthier relationships for yourself.

COACHING ACTION

To begin to uncover your relationship themes, reflect upon and ask yourself the following questions:

1. Do I fear I will be left, so I leave first? Have others left me in my life (parents, other relationships), so I don't trust that my partners will stay?
2. Am I afraid I will fail in relationships, so I don't stay around long enough to find out if I will fail?
3. Do I set such high expectations for my partner that they could never live up to them?
4. Do I have a story that there will always be someone better out there?
5. Did I not have any role models, so I say to myself, "How could I ever do this?"
6. Do I simply feel anxious in the beginning of a relationship and I can't even identify why?

Relationship Theme—The Push-Away Tendency

The first theme is responsible for a lot of anxiety in many. You can feel overwhelmed at the beginning of a relationship as your old fears resurface. You may feel vulnerable and unsafe. You may feel overwhelmed, especially when someone really wants to love you. As a result, you may end up pushing people away. It is a common tendency for someone to push good people away. You can only love someone to the extent you love yourself.

If you are someone who easily feels fear and you have a challenging time staying in relationships because you begin to feel very overwhelmed, it is important to realize:

- You are not this fear.
- You can only love someone to the extent you can love yourself. This means when your self-love hits its limit, you will want to push other people away.
- Continue your self-love work and take care of you.
- As you work to understand who you are, you begin to trust yourself, and you feel safer knowing you can take care of you.
- You will then have less anxiety—that comes from old fear of being hurt—about being in relationships.
- As you grow in your own self-love, you will be able to allow others to love you at a deeper level.

Know you *can* change these patterns. It may take time, but I am living proof that it works.

COACHING ACTION

Here are strategies to assist with staying in relationships, if this is what you want.

1. Be aware of this pattern of fear.
2. Breathe, focus on taking care of yourself, and do not put all your eggs in this relationship basket. Cultivate other relationships which can help you to feel balanced and safer.
3. Let any current or future partners know about this fear that can arise in you. I did this with my husband. He is a nurse anesthetist, so he joked he could give me some medication for this.
4. Take relationships slowly. Take breaks to do your own work to love yourself deeper (do this while in the relationship by taking time for you), and then be with this person again. It is a healing process.

SHARING MY STORY
My Boyfriend Who Lived in Sweden

When I met my husband, he lived in Sweden and I lived in the US. For two full years, we spent three to four weeks together and then spent four to five weeks apart. This arrangement was best for me. When I first met him, I was still unable to handle any more time together. I needed to learn to trust him. After he would leave, I would reflect upon where I had been triggered with him and what this reaction I had was telling me. I used the time apart to continue doing my own self-healing work, which was crucial for me.

I can now thankfully report we are married and all is going well. I had to ease into it and learn to trust him fully. My example shows there is no perfect relationship path or model. The best way to a successful relationship is whatever works for you. Some of us need to ease into relationships more than others in order to ensure success.

Relationship Theme—The Over-Protective "Critical Guard"

This next theme goes into greater detail on one of the push-away tendencies. My definition for the Critical Guard is an actual part of the psyche that acts as a guard. This guard assesses your environment for threats and danger. It is especially alert when you are close with someone because this guard immediately feels you may be in danger due to your past experiences. When the guard senses potential danger, you become more reactive to others. You know the guard is active when you judge others, criticize others, and undermine relationships with others in some way.

Your guard stands before you assessing and criticizing the behavior of others in order to keep you safe. If you have a strong Critical Guard, at some point in your life, typically during childhood, you experienced deep pain. You may have grown up in any of the following family situations; physical abuse, emotional abuse, sexual abuse, family addiction, deaths of loved ones, stressful divorce, family members with mental illness, violence, high conflict, or a prolonged absence of your parents at crucial points in your development.

As a result of these situations, your Critical Guard was developed to help you never feel that pain again. The guard now judges, assesses, and criticizes others first so you won't get hurt. The guard may not want to accept others into your life because it feels it is more important to protect you and keep you safe. A strong Critical Guard may even shut others out of your life in order to keep you unharmed.

The problem occurs when the guard takes care of you as if you are still a child though you are an adult and can keep yourself safe. Like an overprotective mother, the guard does not allow you to experience life. This is a crucial relationship theme to identify. If the Critical Guard runs the show, you may never allow yourself to be in a relationship or create healthy relationships. An over-reactive Critical Guard actually lowers the amount of love we have in our lives.

The key is to love yourself and develop trust in who you are. Once you trust yourself to keep you safe and make healthy choices, your Critical Guard can take a backseat and allow you to drive. You will then be able to attract and sustain healthy love in your life.

COACHING ACTION

1. Take two deep breaths. Close your eyes if you want.
2. Ask yourself: *Do I have a Critical Guard who keeps me safe, keeps others out of my life, or tries to protect me by criticizing/finding fault with others?*
3. Ask yourself: *What has this cost me in my life?*
4. Now, ask your Critical Guard to come and stand in front of you. See her standing there. What is her emotion? Fear, frustration, sadness, indignation, stubbornness, or anger?
5. Ask: *What message do you have for me? Why do you feel this?*
6. Ask: *What can I do to better take care of you? How can I help you trust me to keep us safe?*

7. Ask: *How can we work together to allow love and healthy relation-ships into my life?*
8. Ask: *Is there anything else I need to do?*

Ways to Tame Your Critical Guard:
- Acknowledge your Guard is there, love them, and accept them so they can rest easier.
- Reassure them, tell your Guard you are okay, you are an adult, you have grown up and can take care of yourself.
- Look for the best in others.
- Focus on healing your heart and loving yourself.
- Find your peaceful place if you feel hurt by someone. Don't lash out at others; take care of yourself.
- Believe others are doing their best.
- Lower your expectations (if you have been told you have high expectations) of yourself and others.
- Practice positive self-talk.
- Watch for the guard to show up when you have close re-lationships.
- Watch for signs of your Critical Guard, e.g., shallow breathing, anger, frustration, and other physical reac-tions.
- Verbally tell your Critical Guard to back off.

Prayer to Critical Guard:

Dear Critical Guard,

I know my heart has been hurt in the past. I know your job is difficult, always being on guard. It takes a lot of energy from both of us. I ask you to allow me to love in this lifetime. I ask you to let me make mistakes. I ask you not to be critical of me or those in my life. The peo-ple I choose to have in my life are good. I have grown and will know when a relationship is not healthy for me. When I am critical of others, it only causes problems in the relationship. I love those in my life and I do not need to constantly assess them. I thank you for all the work you have done in the past. However, I ask you to take a backseat now (I will even buckle you in safely), believe in me, and take deep breaths. The road we are on now is a fun rollercoaster, not a dangerous ride.

Relationship Theme—Over-Reaction to Criticism: The Fragile Ego Syndrome

Another theme similar, but not exactly the same, to the Critical Guard is operating from a very fragile ego. This theme is very important to address because for some of you it causes issues in your relationships. Some of you take it personally when you feel you are criticized. I know I react to what I believe is criticism very negatively.

One evening, as I shut the window, my partner commented, "You certainly shut that hard enough." My reaction was one of immediately moving into a defensive position of anger.

What is it about someone saying something to us that can trigger such a deep reaction? I do not now know where the reactions originate, but I am sure they linger from our childhood. I told my partner he seemed like a reprimanding parent at times.

We may have developed oversensitivity to other people's words due to feeling criticized ourselves as a child. If we did not have the love, safety, and security we fully needed in our adolescence, we most likely grew up extremely fragile. We are trying to protect our delicate self, but we end up over-reacting to our partners, children, co-workers, and bosses. I call this the Fragile Ego Syndrome.

To see this pattern is crucial as it is challenging for people with these behaviors to create and sustain healthy relationships. You may defend your Fragile Ego against your partner instead of loving them. Your partner may feel they can't express themselves because you will have a negative reaction to whatever they say. Over time, they tire of this behavior, which can lead to the relationship ending.

When we react from our Fragile Ego, it usually goes like this:

Event →	Fragile Ego Reaction→	Feelings →	Ego Reaction
Sally says something I feel is critical (later when you talk to her she says she did not mean it in a critical way, but you took it that way).	I am not safe with her. This means she does not love me, I am not lovable or worthy. I am alone.	Anger Sadness Rejection Hurt	I will be angry with her, yell, protect myself from her stress response. I think, "She doesn't love me. She is a jerk. I must protect myself."

Let's try option 2. Thankfully, there is always another option. As an adult you can choose how something impacts you in your life.

Event	Ego Reacts	Awareness— Stop.	Choice / Response
Sally says something I feel is critical (when you talk to her later she says she did not mean it in any critical way, but you took it that way).	I am not safe with her. This means she does not love me, I am not lovable or worthy. I am angry. I am alone.	As soon as you feel your hurt feelings you must reflect: I am the person hurting myself. I am angry at myself or others. I am rejecting myself. Sally just said something I thought was critical. I have a choice on how to react to this.	I quickly see the old cycle. I choose how I treat myself and others. I choose to respond, not to react. Sally is not trying to hurt me. She may be in pain; she is stating her opinion. Go to my place of peace and calm. I make a decision from a peaceful place. I respond calmly.

It is usually so automatic, we often think we have no choice in the matter of feeling sad or angry. This may have been the automatic behavior for the caregivers who were our models. Our caregivers may not have known they had a choice not to be angry or sad. You *do* have a choice.

You are an intelligent and amazing human being, and you have the freedom to choose how to react. This upset is not caused by anyone else; you are the one making a choice whether or not to be upset. This is ultimate freedom. It is an amazing thing when you realize this fact.

The Fragile Ego operates only out of fear. It is afraid you will be hurt. You must remember you are an adult now and can keep yourself safe. Remember, you are pure love at your core and pure love does not react to old patterns or fears. Close your eyes and tell yourself, "I love you, beautiful one. I am here loving you and taking care of you."

COACHING ACTION

Step 1:   Ask yourself honestly:
          Do I sometimes overreact to others?
          Do I believe I have a Fragile Ego?

Step 2:   Ask yourself the following questions and listen for the response or write out the response.

          Fragile Ego, why do you get so upset so easily?

          Fragile Ego, what are you most scared of?

          How can I build you up in a healing and loving way to make you stronger?

          What can I do to help you feel safe?

Step 3:   What do I know I need to do differently in my relationships relating to my reactions to others?

Step 4: Say this now, *Fragile Ego, I love you and I am here to keep you safe. Others cannot hurt us with their words or actions. They cannot get to us; we are safe. If they are not being kind we will calmly let them know. Many times, they are just expressing their opinion. If they are continuously unkind, we can leave the relationship. You become unkind to them and me when you get so angry. Let's work together to practice kindness to ourselves and others. We deserve this.*

Relationship Theme—The Coffee Shop Woman—Not Being Responsible

As I wrote this section, I was in a coffee shop sitting next to two women. They were talking so loudly I could not help but overhear them, and I had forgotten my headset. Perfect, of course.

One woman was upset about everything in her life. She went from one story to the next about how others were wronging her or making her life terrible. First, it was her roommate, then it was her co-worker, and next it was her in-laws. I heard absolutely no accountability on her part.

I encourage you to look deeply at your future conversations. Are you like this woman I witnessed in the coffee shop? We need to be mindful of how we allow others to impact us and remember to look at our role in the situation.

COACHING ACTION

1. Where do you put the accountability on others or your partner?
2. Where do you see you could be taking more responsibility in your relationships?

Relationship Theme—The Dangerous Relationship

One man I dated as I began this path of self-love lived his life on the edge. He was hit by boats, surfed at the edge of the boat literally, drove his Harley Davidson motorcycle after drinking, and so forth. When I was with him, there was a part of me that felt so alive living on the edge. However, at one point, when I stood on the cliff and looked over, I decided the kinds of risks he took were too great for me. I realized I was putting my life in jeopardy in various ways by being with him. It was not worth the cost. I did learn a lot about loving myself from this guy. I learned to stand up for myself, love myself, and leave the relationship.

There is a very fine line between living on the edge in a healthy way versus not valuing yourself and your life. If you are in a situation where you and/or someone else are not valuing your life, take a look to see if you have crossed the line where the cliff's edge could start to crumble. Once you assess this, you can make decisions in your best interest. Some people are put in our lives to wake us up.

You may have grown up in an environment where one or more of your parents allowed the other parent to live on this dangerous edge. When you live this reality as a child, you sometimes are not able to easily recognize when you are repeating this pattern. As an adult, you must look deeper and make healthy choices for yourself and your current or future children. Take a moment and consider whether or not you are in this unhealthy cycle. I believe you have the skills and can get the support to do what is necessary to let go of this relationship if that is what is healthy for you. If you are reading this book, I know you are very strong deep down inside.

The bottom line is if someone does not value their life, they cannot value you right now. It is that simple. If you now realize your partner is not valuing their life, you have some choices to make. Others get to choose how to live their lives; you get to choose to be involved with them or not.

COACHING ACTION

Ask yourself the following questions to determine if you are too close to the edge in any relationship:

1. Does your partner (or the person in question) truly value their life?
2. Have they put your (or your children's) life or livelihood (income that supports you) at risk in a big way?
3. Do you find yourself taking risks that are life threatening (or threatening to your livelihood) as a result of being in this relationship?
4. Have others who you know love you voiced their concern about this relationship to you?
5. Are you truly respecting yourself and your values by staying in this relationship?

Relationship Theme—Not Being In Relationships

Some of you may choose to heal primarily on your own. This can be a wonderful and very effective approach, but there is a caveat I must mention. Do not take excessive time by yourself *if* you want a partner one day. You can heal while you are solo, but the only way to uncover certain emotional pain you have buried is to be in a relationship, which will allow you to refine your skills. A relationship is a perfect way to have your wounds and needs reflected back to you.

I know people who choose not to be in a relationship, which is fine if they don't have a goal of ever being in a partnership. If you really want a life partner, it is best to take the risk on relationships and see what shows up. If you stay wrapped in your own safe cocoon solo you will not learn the lessons relationships are here to teach you.

When I was single for many years in my thirties, I made a conscious decision to have a roommate so I could practice living with someone in a relationship. When I was a child, there had been so much conflict in my family that living with others actually created anxiety for me. In my twenties, I had been unsuccessful with roommates; I did not have the skills. Once I had learned enough skills, I used roommates to learn how to work through the conflict and anxiety in myself that always showed up for me in my relationships.

They allowed me to learn how to live and interact more peacefully with others. I knew having roommates would allow me to continue to learn skills to live more easily with a partner one day. My plan was a success; my husband and I live together very well overall. I also know some people who have gotten so set in their ways living alone that it would be almost impossible for them to allow a partner into their lives, even though that is what they still say they want.

I encourage you to take the chance and be in relationships. Remember, no matter what happens, you will always learn a lot about yourself. I can promise you this.

COACHING ACTION

1. Say the following to yourself: *I am open to accepting the perfect relationship to assist me in my healing, so I may grow to be successful in all of my relationships. I am grateful. I trust myself enough to take a chance on a relationship.*
2. If you choose, write the following and post it where you will see it: *I will commit to a healthy, loving relationship by* (insert date).
3. What do you know you need to do (what steps do you need to take) to have a healthy and loving relationship in your life?

Relationship Theme—Being Over-Responsible for Others / Codependency

Many of you have the tendency to want to be caretakers of others. You believe you ultimately are responsible for the health and happiness of others. The truth is other people must want to be happy and healthy on their own. We try to assist them, and if they don't want to move ahead, we get tired and worn down trying to help them. This was my normal mode in relationships. I was always the caretaker, trying to make others happy—my version of their happiness. You cannot make someone else happy; they must do it themselves. You must learn instead to love yourself first and foremost.

As I said, my pattern in relationships was always trying to assist others in being happy. I learned this from being a kid caught in the middle of two feuding and unhappy parents. I wanted to be able to fix everything. I wanted things to work. I wanted us all to be happy. I had no idea how to make this happen in my family. However, I still felt responsible for doing this. While I journeyed through life, I dragged this old garbage with me. I felt responsible for others' happiness, I wanted them to be okay, even though most of the time I was not happy. I have learned I'm not responsible for someone else's happiness or success. I can only focus on me.

In your adult relationships, when you believe you have to be responsible and take care of others, *you actually take away their power.* You are passively telling them they are not strong and need you to take care of them. This will keep them weak. You disempower them because they cannot feel strong and confident if you are always taking care of or controlling them or the situation. This pattern can show up in all your relationships including partners, children, and co-workers.

There is a fine line here. The line is the difference between *supporting* someone to be healthy and strong or *enabling* them to remain sick or disempowered. Supporting someone is telling them they must go to rehab before they can remain with you and your kids. Enabling someone is allowing them to drink and covering for them because you feel responsible to take care of them. Clearly, you are not helping them by enabling them. It is crucial to be clear on this because when you are enabling someone there always is an imbalance of power. Power imbalance does not create a healthy relationship.

In codependent relationships, there is the enabler and the enabled. Neither role is healthy. Some people end up feeling they can't exist without the other person, and that creates a negative relationship dynamic. It can be especially tough when they separate. If you feel you have this need to assist others at a very deep level and you almost lose yourself in taking care of someone else, I recommend reading additional resources on codependency to understand it better. I have some recommendations in the reference section. You may also want to work with a professional to assist you if you believe this is something that challenges you.

Another important point to realize is if you are always trying to make others happy, you don't have to take the time to focus on your own issues. Helping others excessively can be a distraction for you, so you don't have to focus on you.

If you are someone who is always trying to assist others, this is a clue that your true path is to assist yourself in loving **you** more deeply. Let go of the old need to help others right now. This won't help you. You can be an amazing influence and guide in the world without having to help others all the time.

If you stop focusing on being responsible for others, your strength will double as the weight of the world is magically removed from your shoulders.

Once you develop your own self-love, you will empower others versus enabling them to stay small.

COACHING ACTION

1. Is there anyone in your life for whom you are too responsible?
2. Can you see how taking care of or controlling this person negatively impacts you, them, and the relationship?
3. What can you do to give them their power back and see them as strong?
4. What do you need to do to take better care of yourself instead of focusing on others?

Affirmation

Dear Higher Power,

Allow me to know that at the depth of my soul, my first responsibility is to myself. Allow me to let go of any pressure I place on myself, consciously or unconsciously, to be responsible for others' happiness. I thank you for allowing me to shine my light in the world and not be responsible for the world.

COACHING ACTION

Our relationships provide us so much information. Reflect on your past or present romantic, professional, or personal relationships. What happened or is happening in those relationships? On a piece of paper, write your answers to the questions below for three of your relationships. The goal here is to see themes in your relationships.

1. What did this person not provide (or is not providing) that you want from them?
2. What were/are your frustrations in the relationship?
3. What were/are your partner's/other person's frustrations in the relationship?
4. Are you/did you stay too long?
5. If the relationship/partnership ended, why did it end?
6. Who was responsible for it ending?
7. Who was to blame? Why?

After doing this for three relationships, ask yourself:

1. Do you see any patterns in these relationships?
2. What insights do you have as you consider all three of these relationships?
3. Is there anything you want to be responsible for?

Creating your future relationships:

1. What new patterns do you want to create in relationships?
2. How do you want to act in the relationship?
3. What type of person do you want to bring into your life?

Summary

Relationships are a plethora of information. If you pay attention, you can alter the course of your life. They show you things you could never have figured out on your own. No matter how hard or challenging they seem at the time, every relationship—current and past—is a gift to you to ensure you have the data you need to understand how to love yourself better.

THE MANY GIFTS OF RELATIONSHIPS

*Relationships can be challenging, but if you take the time to
find the gifts of relationships, you have the opportunity to grow
toward your ultimate potential.*

Gift of Relationship—Lesson 1: The People We (Somehow) Choose

We choose others to assist us in working through our own
life issues, pain, or trauma. Do I think we consciously do this? No
way, but it happens. I am a researcher at heart, and I have seen this
phenomenon often in my own life and in the lives of so many others.
I choose to believe it is our need to heal past pain that draws us to
these specific individuals.

Many therapists, including me, believe we are attracted to
others with a similar level of wounding. In my work over the past
twelve years with so many families of divorce and high conflict, I
have worked with hundreds of very dysfunctional couples. Often one
person will come to me and say how bad the other person is. I know
deep down that the person who is telling me the other person is crazy
has all of his/her own issues. The truth is if someone tells me their
partner is crazy, I know in some way they themselves are also challenged at a very deep level.

Sometimes one person realizes how dysfunctional the relationship is and leaves. This is certainly a step on that person's path to

self-love. However, at one point she/he was once as unhealthy as the other person was. This is what attracted them, even if they married the person because they thought they could help this other person. A person who marries someone to help a very unhealthy person is also an unhealthy person. As we discussed in the last chapter, this is called codependency and enabling of others. No matter how unhealthy your partner or past partners may seem, you must take responsibility for the fact that, at one point, you chose them.

At some level, we are still working to heal wounds from our childhood. As an example, my first fiancé was emotionally distant. That felt safe and normal to me because I had grown up with a father who never hugged me or told me he loved me. As I grew and trusted my fiancé more, I wanted more from him, but he was unable to provide more physical and emotional support. I became frustrated and finally ended the relationship. Again, I had chosen him. We choose others because some familiarity from our past caregivers draws us to them. It is this same familiarity that, in some cases, splits us apart.

We don't consciously choose a relationship based on this similarity to our caregivers, it chooses us. It is a subconscious pattern, an imprint from our caregivers we are not consciously aware of. In some cases, this imprint carries our deepest wounding. When two people are attracted to each other, many times it is due to the deep pain they both have experienced in their lives. The gift is that through the relationship we can heal this old hurt in various ways.

COACHING ACTION

1. Look back at your most challenging relationship. Can you see how choosing this person was somehow related to the relationships you saw or were a part of as a child?

2. What healing do you know you need to do when you look at your own pattern or part in this challenging relationship?

Gift of Relationship—Lesson 2: How Others Assist You to Love Yourself More

This phenomenon of attracting others into your life who assist in your healing is nothing short of amazing. I know sometimes it does not feel that way. I am so grateful for all the men in my life who have taught me so much through many of my failed relationships. Failure is our best teacher. If we can learn from the relationship, it is a cause for celebration. I once dated a man who I thought I loved so much, but it was not love.

After the relationship ended, I began referring to him as the self-love teacher for women because after he and I completed our relationship, he dated two other women I knew, and he seemed to teach all of us how to better love ourselves. He did not treat any of us well, but we were so attracted to him and his unloving behaviors. He was there as our teacher, so we could all realize we needed to love ourselves deeper.

This healing path can take time and it can be frustrating. Once I decided to love myself, I seemed to attract even worse partners into my life. It did not seem fun, and it was confusing, but they all taught me so much. I somehow had thought once I realized I needed to love myself my perfect partner would magically appear. In some way, he did. A healthy partnership could not happen until I learned to be my own loving partner. Slowly, but surely, one by one, the men I dated taught me all the lessons I needed to learn. They were all more than happy to help me. I was like a sitting duck just waiting for them to choose me. I think I must have had "I need self-love teaching" written on my forehead. I was on a fast track, and it truly felt like baptism by fire for a few years. However, the self-love I have now was completely worth those frustrating days. Be patient. It took me many years of learning about self-love and studying myself and others in order to write this book.

COACHING ACTION

1. Who have been your self-love teachers? They can be parents, others in your life, past partners, or current partners.
2. Close your eyes and take a deep breath.
3. Envision one of them in your mind. Feel your emotions.
4. Now ask each one of them, "What were/are you teaching me about self-love?"
5. Envision them again, forgive them, and thank them.

Gift of Relationship—Lesson 3: Soul Mates & Journey Buddies

A word now on soul mates: A client of mine once had a spiritual teacher who told him a man in his life was his soul mate. Due to my client's definition, he believed he was destined to be with this man forever. I disagree. To me, a soul mate is someone or something that comes in and touches our life in a deep and meaningful way. They do not actually have to be with us for a long period of time. They profoundly impact the course of our soul and the path of our life. We also can have animal soul mates. I believe we also have short-term soul mates which, due to my path, I call Journey Buddies.

Our soul mates do not have to be our life partner. They do not even have to be with us for a long time. No matter what amount of time we spend with them, they touch us at a deep level, a level we have never felt before. They allow us to access a place inside ourselves we have not accessed before. This is my definition of a true soul mate. I believe my beloved Shih Tzu, Sassy Girl, who just passed and journeyed with me for twelve years as my furry companion, was an animal soul mate for me. This beautiful dog taught me so much.

During the time I wrote this book, I realized my short-term soul mates came into my life, created a lot of commotion, and left again. I was usually highly attracted to these people, but for whatever reason, we did not spend a long time together. Still, the time we spent together felt very compressed and the lessons I learned were intense.

After a few of these relationships, I realized each of these people were my soul mates, they were just not meant to be my life partner. It was as if we had agreed to come together in this lifetime to help me learn a very important self-love lesson. A short-term soul mate (Journey Buddy) or animal soul mate is just as capable as a long-term soul mate of allowing us to learn, grow, and find our deep self-love. Sometimes our greatest healing can come from these relationships.

However, we sometimes get wrapped up in believing we have to find that one soul mate. It is very important not to judge yourself if you do not have a long-term soul mate at this time. Being married for the first time at forty-two, short-term soul mates and animal soul mates each played a crucial role in my self-love journey.

SHARING MY STORY
Short-Term Soul Mate in Peru

Carlos is the short-term soul mate (Journey Buddy) who stands out the most for me. He was from Brazil. We crossed paths in Peru on a boat trip to Taquile Island where we were going to do a homestay with a family. We had an instant connection. When the trip ended, we gave each other our necklaces as we parted. I still have his.

Later in my trip, I crossed the mountains on a night bus to see him again. After an eight-hour, freezing cold bus ride, I arrived in Cusco at 6:00 a.m. It was a miracle (we did not have cell phones!) that he was there with open arms to greet me lovingly. When I stepped off the bus, I saw him waiting there for me as he promised, and I received his loving embrace. I was engulfed by a level of trust I had never felt before with another man. I will never forget the moment of being a stranger in a foreign land, greeted by my loving friend. People saw us together and thought we were newlyweds even though we'd only been together a few days. We were happy together; I was radiant with love. The love he shared with me was deep and special.

When it was time to return home, it felt like my heart was breaking. As he left me at the airport, I wept like I never had before because the love I felt was nothing I had permitted myself to experience before due to my old fears. The tears were deep tears of old sorrow and grief that were able to be released through his loving kindness. The relationship broke my heart open in a very positive way.

Though it was not meant to continue, it provided me with a deeper knowledge of what love really felt like. It also healed some old wounds in a way I cannot explain. He will always hold a special place in my heart.

My experience made it clear to me that many people can be our soul mates. Not all are meant to journey with us for a lifetime. However, when we decide to enter into a long-term relationship with someone, this is our soul mate, as well. No matter what the outcome of this longer relationship is, we decide to learn important lessons from and with this person. I continue to learn all the time about myself in my relationship with my husband. To be clear, your self-love journey continues even as you are in a long-term partnership.

The bottom line is this: you receive some very deep healing through your connection, short- or long-term, with this other person. They will always play a role in impacting your self-love. They are here as your teachers and guides, guides to teach you about your inner self.

COACHING ACTION

1. Looking back on your life, who have your soul mates or journey buddies been and what did they teach you?
2. Make a list of those who have come into your life, even if only for a short time, to provide you with much-needed guidance, love, or maybe even rejection and pain.
3. What are you grateful for that they gave you?

Gift of Relationship—Lesson 4: When Someone Leaves You

One of my honored guides and teachers was Mattie J.T. Stepanek. I saw this loving child at the Mall of America in Minneapolis.

I did not even know who he was at the time, but he captured my attention. His body was so weak, but his beautiful, angelic spirit filled the room. Mattie inspired me. That day, I bought his book, *Journey through Heartsongs*. He began writing poetry at three. He touched many people with his presence and love for the world. Mattie passed away at the age of thirteen (he had the same illness as his brother in his poem below). The poem, reprinted with permission, is a beautiful example of how we can feel we are at fault if someone leaves us. In most cases, as in Mattie's, that is the furthest thing from the truth.

Unanswered Questions

My brother, Jamie died.
His muscles—and—bones
Did not work at all anymore.
His happiness and specialness
Went into Heaven and
His body got buried in
The hole that goes into the ground
And then into the sky and
And then to the Everywhere
And Forever that is Heaven.
I know why he died,
But I also don't know why.
I really don't.
He is happy,
And sometimes I am, too.
And sometimes I am sad
Or angry or scared or confused.
And sometimes I think
That maybe,
I didn't hold his hand tight enough.

~ December 1993

Some of us have a difficult time letting relationships go. You may feel you have failed and you feel you could have done more or made better choices. You feel as if you did not get something right and there is something not right within you.

Many times, it is not about you. I believe the person who is leaving the relationship or who does not want to partake in the relationship fully is the person who many times needs more time to grow. The person left behind sometimes thinks, "What is wrong with me?" or "Why don't they love me?" It was not that you did not hold their hand tight enough, as Mattie thought in this poem. Sometimes you simply loved them and they needed to leave to continue their growth. You do not get to make yourself wrong for not loving them enough. You did all you could with the resources and skills you had at the time.

COACHING ACTION

1. Is there any relationship in which you still feel that somehow you did not hold their hand tight enough?
2. Breathe into any pain you may feel. Just allow any pain to surface.
3. See this person in front of you now. Tell them anything you need to say to them. Get it all out. Feel any feelings you may have buried.
4. Listen for anything they would want to say to you now. Imagine them forgiving you and telling you what they need to say.
5. Envision yourself holding their hand and then let their hand go and thank them for all they gave you (physically hold your hand like you are holding theirs and then take your hand back into your body, letting go of their hand). Breathe deep. Let go and say to yourself: *I did all that I could with the skills I had at the time, I forgive myself.*

Gift of Relationship—Lesson 5: Healing After the Death of a Partner, Parent, or Significant Other

There is another phenomenon I have witnessed in relationships. When there is a death of a partner, parent, or significant other, sometimes the person who passes has been a great caretaker or source of security for the other person. In this case, the person left behind sometimes has a lot of self-love work to do. When their partner or another significant person in their life passes, it is extremely difficult for them. They have many fears about their ability or desire to face life alone. I believe the love they received from this now departed person laid the foundation for them to face their deepest fears and deeply love themselves.

In the end, every person I have seen this happen to always learns to love themselves in some deeper, more beautiful way. However, they never would have had the opportunity to do this crucial self-love work here on Earth if this other person had outlived them.

Any relationship ending can be seen in this light. We can see their love as a gift that can never be taken from us. It is a gift they have given us for the rest of our life. It's part of who we are, forever.

COACHING ACTION

1. Think of anyone who has passed away during your life.
2. What might their passing have taught you about self-love?
3. Envision the love you received from them deep in your heart and body, feel this love, breathe deeply into this love. This love is forever yours.
4. Listen to any messages they may want to give you right now about love.
5. Ask them, "What do I need to do to bring more love into my life?"
6. Ask them anything else you want to and listen to what they have to say.

7. Thank them for all they gave you. Once again, feel the beautiful love they gave you. Breathe deeply into this love.

Gift of Relationship—Lesson 6: Conquer Fear of Commitment

Fear of commitment can arise from many places:

- A lack of connection or lacking a safe connection with your own parents or caregivers.
- Someone leaving you (a death or ending of a relationship).
- You feeling you have failed in relationships in the past.

When you fear commitment, you may find yourself always looking for an excuse to not be in a relationship or stay in a relationship. You are always looking for the exit door, so you can have a "valid" reason to jump ship at any point. Usually, if this is your pattern, you have some subconscious story you are carrying around.

SHARING MY STORY
Fear of Commitment

At one point when I realized I was a commitment-phobic person, I started dating someone new. I decided I was going to fully accept him and commit to the relationship. After I did, I learned he was still legally married to his "ex," as he had called her. He had not lived with her for years, but he was still legally married. That tested my commitment promise. I stayed in the relationship and I set boundaries about what I would tolerate. He legally divorced and we learned quite a bit from each other. I also learned a lot from his ex-wife with whom he had a child. She was a frightening woman to me and the drama she created reminded me of my own family growing up. I firmly believe I attracted that situation into my life to heal those old wounds from my own parents' divorce and finally set healthy boundaries for myself.

We never know what gifts lay in our relationships when we *fully* commit to them. This relationship ended once he became clear he did not want to be a father again. However, because I chose to commit and stay in it when it got tough, I learned a lot about myself.

COACHING ACTION

Take some time to reflect on the questions below. Simply uncovering a belief can create a shift in your life and relationships.

1. Do I fear I will be left, so I leave first?
2. Am I afraid I will fail in a relationship, so I do not stay around long enough to find out if I will fail?
3. Do I set such high expectations for a partner that they could never be reached?
4. Do I have a story that there will always be someone better out there?
5. Have others left me in my life (parents, other relationships), so I don't trust that anyone will stay?
6. Did my parents struggle in their relationship, so I say, "How could I ever do this?"

Now ask yourself these questions:

1. What do you know you need to do to accept relationships into your life?
2. What do you know you need to do differently to commit more fully to your next relationship or your current relationship?
3. What do you want to commit to in your next relationship or current relationship?

Gift of Relationship—Lesson 7: The End of Relationships and Anger/Sadness

If you are still angry or sad about a past relationship, romantic or other, for any reason, this is a gift. It says you have more healing to do. Anger or sadness at someone who has left you, either through the end of a relationship or death, serves a purpose. This anger or sadness is the last thing connecting you to them. You fear, often subconsciously, that if you let this emotional connection go, you will forever lose this other person. The irony is if you hang onto this anger or sadness, you may lose out on your capacity to love anyone fully.

You may need to look deeply at why you are hanging onto anger or sadness, and this is not always fun. However, in the end, it will be worth every painful minute when you understand why you are choosing to stay stuck in anger and/or sadness. Once you are able to release the anger and/or sadness, you will love yourself and those around you more deeply. You may also want to seek support in this process. It can be a challenge to see the forest through the trees when you are looking at your deep issues. Coaches, therapists, and other trained professionals can assist with this if needed.

COACHING ACTION

Step 1:   Do you have anger or sadness about a past relationship?

Step 2:   Take a few deep breaths, get quiet, close your eyes, and ask yourself:

- Why am I still holding onto this pain?
- Is there any part of me that thinks I don't deserve to be happy?
- What one thing can I do to move forward from this pain?
- What choice do I need to make to allow myself to live a happy life?

Gift of Relationship—Lesson 8: Relationship Completion

Completion means you make a choice to acknowledge your part in the end of the relationship and you do something that symbolizes letting the relationship go. When you complete your relationship, you should say the truth for yourself, and take responsibility. An example is, "I did not really know you when we became intimate, but I chose to be with you. We created a child together and I take responsibility for that." Normally, you are not forced into a relationship. You are an adult with your own free will. Once you take responsibility for your part, you can complete any messes you have made with others. You can honor the other person. You can possibly even express to them the gifts they gave you and thank them. If someone has left you, this may not seem possible, but it truly is.

When we officially take the time to complete a relationship, we are able to release some attachment to it. Sometimes, you may not even have to speak with the person; you can write a letter and not send it. You can also create a ritual or event symbolizing the end of the relationship. Once you complete the relationship, you are now free to move on. It may also be that when you let go of the attachment, the relationship is free to grow in ways you could not have imagined. I cannot stress enough the importance of completion. I encourage you to complete it in some way, even if it is hard. In the end, it will be more difficult if you choose *not* to go through this process. Completions provide something beneficial for both parties involved.

SHARING MY STORY
My First Love Completion Story

I am going to share one of my most recent and most painful completion stories. We can each choose to complete our relationship in our own way. I challenge you as you read this story to think about the relationships in your life you still need to fully complete. My soul mate, Andy, my first love in college whom I could not love at the

115

time (the story I shared earlier in this book), came back into my life a few years ago. This was twelve years after the last time I had seen him. I had flown to Colorado to complete our first relationship of five years and say goodbye to him in person. Strangely enough, we both live in Colorado now, only six hours apart.

After years of not being in touch, he contacted me and we met at a marina and then spent two wonderful weekends together. For me, it was pure bliss. I had longed for the opportunity to show him my love. I still loved him so much. He had changed, but the feelings I had for him were unbelievable. I felt I was living in a dream.

Then, as quickly has he had landed back in my life, he left. He told me he could not be with me and gave me no explanation. I thought we were going to be married and have children. It was ironic that, initially, I could not love him and now he could not love me. It was more like a terrible nightmare. I was deeply hurt and angry. I felt like my heart had been ripped out of my chest, the pain was so deep. I wondered how I would love again. I was living alone up in the mountains at that time, in the home I so desperately wanted a partner and children to share with me, and it was a time of profound sorrow.

After a few months, I was still angry with him. A friend asked me, "Why are you still angry?" As I reflected, I knew the resentment was the only thing left holding me to him. If I let it go, I would lose him forever. It was my last and only connection to him. I knew what I needed to do. I had to complete the relationship and let him go. For seventeen years I had carried with me the twenty-four karat, two hearts-entwined earrings he had given me for my college graduation. When he gave them to me, he had said, "Our hearts will be together forever." I also had his favorite hat which he had thrown carelessly into a pile of clothes in my bedroom when he first arrived at my house. I had not realized it was there until weeks later.

I gathered up my lot of memories and I headed down the road in my Subaru to a trailhead. I walked to a clearing in the woods where I could see a beautiful view. First, I dug a hole and buried the earrings and then I made a cross of wood and put it there on top of the hole. I then took his hat and tossed it as far as I could and said, "Goodbye, Andy," thanking him for his love. I cried like a baby— deep, heart-wrenching sobs. I left my anger in the mountains that day. I also left some pain. I forgave him and me. It was better after that. It was far from easy, but I had finally made the choice to let him and the relationship go.

This really helped me move on with life as I was no longer angry with him, but the truth was I still needed answers from him about why this happened. Why had he left my life as quickly as he had come? In a strange turn of events, I needed to attend a class near where he lived in Colorado two and a half years later. I called him and asked him to call me. I did not hear from him, but he knew I was thinking of him. I decided I would stop and see him at his school. I knew where he taught. I left early that morning, so I would time my arrival as his school day was ending. It was a long six-hour drive, but I really needed this for myself. I was very calm and knew in my heart that this was the right thing to do. I showed up at the school, asked the woman at the front desk to talk to him and she told me where his room was. Yes, I know it seems strange, but it all worked perfectly. I remember walking down the hall, feeling like I was on a mission. I needed to complete this in person. I looked into his classroom and made eye contact with his deep brown eyes. He gave me a nod of deep recognition and I motioned that I would wait outside until the end of his class. We could talk to each other without words. College had been hard for him and I was so proud to see him teaching kids. I waited and about fifteen minutes later, which seemed like years, he was ready to talk.

It was a great conversation, with no blame and only peace. He apologized. He shared his current life difficulties. I reminded him of the great guy he was and thanked him for all he had given me so many years earlier. He acknowledged he had loved me when we reunited, but had been in a lot of pain and not ready for a true relationship. I told him how loving myself had been helpful to me in my current relationship (with my now husband). It was probably one of the most healing conversations either of us had ever had. As I left and reflected on this conversation, I realized this completion visit was also for him and his healing, maybe even more for him than me.

I don't think this is necessary for everyone, but I am someone who needs to complete in person when I feel this deeply about someone. That is why this was crucial for me. I am grateful we had two opportunities together to learn about loving ourselves deeper in this life. The love he gave me will be part of my heart forever. I am grateful that because of him and the love he gave me so many years ago I am now able to be the partner and mother I am.

COACHING ACTION

Sometimes having a ritual to complete our relationships is crucial. I ask you to think about your past relationships. Is there anything you need to do to be fully complete?

Relationship Completion Ideas:
- Write a letter to them and symbolically burn it.
- Bury something that was special to you and is symbolic of the relationship.
- Go out with friends and call it your completion get-together.
- Ask the person to complete with them directly, if you both are calm enough for this.
- Create a work of art that symbolizes your new life.
- Create or purchase any symbol that represents the ending of the relationship or the beginning of your new life.

When you do this, focus on:
- What are you letting go of?
- What were the gifts of the relationship?
- What are you creating next in life?

Gift of Relationship—Lesson 9: Relationship Redesign

Once you have completed the relationship, you can look at redesigning the relationship. If you won't see them again, there is no need to redesign. The relationship is concluded with completion and reflection of what the relationship provided to you. If you will still see them, due to common friends or children, redesign is important.

In redesigning, you should come together and talk about what type of contact can work for each of you. This is especially important in divorce situations where children are involved. Kids need two well-adjusted and cooperating parents. The process of redesigning together can be extremely empowering for everyone involved. This process will take a bit of communication, but I know you are up for the challenge. As I have grown in my own self-love and confidence, I have been able to peacefully redesign every important romantic relationship that has ended. Once you do your own processing and healing around the relationship, there is just truly no reason you should not be able to be friends or at least be civil with this person. They played an important role in your life; they just did not end up being your life partner. If you are able to complete with someone, it shows you have done your own work and your life moves on.

COACHING ACTION

Here are questions for redesigning your relationship:

1. Do we want to interact? How do we want to interact? Do we have to interact?
2. What agreements can we make about how we will communicate? How can we be sure this is respectful to both of us?
3. Can I respect this person for the simple reason they are human, too and we all make mistakes?

4. What do I want to be responsible for regarding this relationship, our issues, or the ending? This should be simple.

5. I commit to _____ (what can you do to ensure a peaceful future existence with this person). Both of you fill in this blank in writing and then say it aloud.

6. Both of you simply say to the other, "I am grateful for the learning I received from this relationship. I am complete. Thank you."

Summary

A relationship is a true gift. Take time now to thank your Higher Power for all the relationships that have given you so many gifts of love. Remember you have been a gift to many others, as well. Thank yourself for all the failures and successes you have achieved.

HEALTHY RELATIONSHIPS THROUGH
BOUNDARIES, SAFETY, AND TRUST

Feeling safe and acting in ways that create safety for others is at the heart of healthy relationships. Setting healthy boundaries or limits is a crucial aspect of feeling safe in a relationship. When you feel safe and secure, healthy relationships are the result.

The truth is you may not consciously realize when your boundaries are being crossed in an unhealthy way or when you are crossing others' boundaries in an unhealthy way because that is all you have ever experienced. You may have grown up in an environment with unhealthy boundaries where you did not feel fully safe. Examples of these types of environments include: emotional, physical, verbal, and sexual abuse; high-conflict parents; family members with mental illness; or parents who were not available to you and did not teach you how to thrive by setting good boundaries. You may have been in a situation where your boundaries were continuously violated, often without you even realizing it. Even if your parents did everything for you and/or allowed you to do whatever you wanted, they also modeled unhealthy boundaries to you.

The good news is you can learn to set healthy boundaries as an adult. To do this, you must first learn how to recognize the signs of unhealthy boundaries in your life. In this chapter, you will look at signs that tell you your boundaries are not healthy. You will also explore how you can create healthy boundaries in your relationships.

To get started identifying and becoming aware of where you may have boundary issues, take a moment to reflect on each of the questions below that could be clues to boundary issues in your life.

1. When do you feel angry with others?
2. When do others get angry with you?
3. Do you live in a constant state of feeling overwhelmed?
4. Do you have trouble saying "no" to others?
5. Do you feel like others drain your energy?
6. Is another person verbally or physically abusive to you?

Many of the feelings and emotions in the statements above are giving you warning signals that your boundaries are not healthy. When your boundaries are weak, unprotected, or unclear, you may end up giving away your own personal power without realizing it. Let's explore what healthy and unhealthy boundaries look like.

Exploring Boundaries—Lesson 1: Anger, Safety, and Boundaries

Anger shows up in two ways to alert you that you may have boundary issues occurring:

1. You may feel anger if you allow your boundaries to be trampled and you feel taken advantage of.
2. You may also feel anger if others do not set healthy boundaries with you, which can leave you feeling unsafe.

As I worked with children, I began to recognize that boundaries, structures, and rules made them (especially kids from unsafe backgrounds) feel safe and secure. What I had not realized is boundaries also make adults feel safe and secure. I saw this play out with one of my adult clients. Her husband did not set boundaries with her. How this looked in their relationship was she walked all over him and was not kind with her words. Her husband would not set a boundary by telling her to stop. When he did not set the healthy boundary for her, she actually felt more unsafe with him (just as kids test us, so we will set safe boundaries with them) and her behavior escalated. Her husband would just leave and be angry with her because she had crossed his boundaries. Then, he would tell her she did not respect him (which was true). However, from my perspective, he did not respect himself enough to tell her to stop early on and set a boundary with her. Of course, my client had work to do; her husband was teaching her. We had to work with her to take care of herself and be responsible for her own behavior and fears. Both she and her husband were exhibiting unhealthy boundary patterns.

Think about your relationships. It may be you have issues trusting others and feeling safe in relationships due to past experiences in which your boundaries were crossed in an unhealthy way. You also may not trust yourself to keep yourself safe or act in a safe manner with others due to an inability to set healthy boundaries.

If there is an area in your life where you feel angry or where you feel someone or some situation takes advantage of you, it may be at work or simply dealing with people, this is a boundary issue.

COACHING ACTION

Ask yourself the following questions to help uncover areas where you may have unhealthy boundaries:

1. Is there anyone you need to walk away from and set boundaries with when their anger or behavior gets to be too much?
2. Is there anyone who gets angry with you and you can see now you may be crossing their boundaries?
3. Is there anyone who gets angry with you and you can now see you are not setting boundaries with them?
4. Is there anyone or any situation you are angry with and you can see that it could be due to a boundary issue?

If you answered yes to any of the above:

1. Take a deep breath, close your eyes, and focus inside of yourself.
2. Connect to your feeling of anger, sadness, or frustration over this situation.
3. Take a deep breath and ask yourself what is this anger, frustration, or sadness telling me? If it had a voice, what would it say right now?
4. Ask, how do I take back my power in this situation?
5. Ask, what one step is crucial for me to take, so I create safety for myself or the other person in this relationship?

Exploring Boundaries—Lesson 2: Overwhelm

Being overwhelmed is a common feeling for many. It shows up when you feel out of control. You may have lived in this state a lot as a child or due to some event in your life. It may now be a pattern in your life. Living in a state of overwhelm is not healthy for us or those around us. The really great news is it's solved best by simply learning to set boundaries with yourself.

Often the person you need to set boundaries with lives inside your mind. You are usually the only one allowing "the overwhelm" to impact you. In my personal experience, working from home and on my own, I had a tendency to live in stress about everything I had to do. It sometimes led me to be unproductive. I have learned to commit to setting reasonable boundaries with myself and others. These boundaries allow me the space to feel calm and clear again.

The truth is, those around you pay for the state of mind you live in through your stress, anger, or frustration. In the end, you pay for it by not being productive (at work) or through loss of love/relationship. It takes you out of living your best life by focusing you on things you really can't control. Doing this can keep you stuck.

When in this disempowered state we are not living in the present. We are worrying about the future or lamenting the past.

The key to managing it is to manage your thoughts. You must catch the thoughts immediately and speak to them, letting them know you are not going to live in this place of fear. By not setting good boundaries with your thoughts, you make yourself feel unsafe. If you set healthy boundaries around your overwhelm, you will be more efficient—by being calmer. You will then be able to more easily complete and manifest the important things in your life. The way to do this is to simply slow down to speed up. That's right, slow down so you can move faster, with a greater purpose in your life. Slowing down allows us to be present with ourselves instead of operating from fear. From this place of safety, we can actually be more productive. We think more clearly from a place of calm presence, even if we feel we are not moving as fast.

COACHING ACTION

Think of the last time you felt overwhelmed.

1. Physically go back to that time (maybe it was sitting at your desk looking at emails, looking around at a messy house, or thinking about all you have to do). Feel the emotions—what did you feel like in that moment?
2. Remember what you were most likely saying to yourself (I can't do this, I can't handle this, I have to do this or there will be a big consequence).
3. When did you feel disempowered as a child?
4. Can you acknowledge you are no longer that young child?
5. What do you think living from this place as an adult creates in your life?
6. What new story do you need to tell yourself when you feel yourself moving into or living in overwhelm?

7. In those moments when overwhelm creeps in, what do you need to do to move back to the present?

Exploring Boundaries—Lesson 3: Energy Drain and Boundaries

Some people seem to drain your energy. The truth is, you *allow* them to drain your energy. When two people engage, and the behavior of one of them really frustrates the other, it creates an energy drain because one person allows themselves to be frustrated by the other person. Some people, due to their level of functioning in life, can seem to drain energy from others. Examples include individuals who always have some issue going on, individuals who are loud and rude, and individuals who get angry easily and are careless with their words. A lot of these behaviors I call *drama*. When people are in drama, they are usually operating from old trauma.

Of course, it is their right to behave this way and you can do little to stop them. However, something may be triggered in you by their behavior. Their drama can even trigger your old trauma if you get sucked into it. This is old unresolved trauma and this person is mirroring something to you. This is what creates a feeling inside of you of your energy being drained.

An example of this was a friend of mine who was frustrated with a woman at a training I attended because the other woman always needed attention and was loud and obnoxious. When I saw this obnoxious woman, I saw a little girl needing attention and I was able to have empathy for her. This woman was a trigger for my friend. I was able to separate myself (boundaries) from the woman and not be drawn into her drama. My friend, however, became extremely frustrated with her. She finally admitted the woman reminded her of her mother. This woman was a trigger for my friend's old, unresolved feelings/trauma and that felt frustrating and tiring to my friend. It felt as if this loud woman was draining her energy, but my friend was draining her own energy being triggered by this woman.

COACHING ACTION

There are two important things you can do once you realize this energy drain is occurring:

1. Look into your own life to see what unresolved issue is being triggered that allows this person to "hook you" and drain your energy. What old trauma or story of yours is pulling you into this place of frustration?
2. If you still feel triggered by this person or situation, set a healthy boundary and remove yourself from the situation or disengage from this person. You may do this physically or energetically in your mind if you can't physically get away from this person's negative energy.

SHARING MY STORY
Family Triggers

One Christmas, I felt my sister started to speak to me very rudely. I became completely hooked, feeling hurt and angry. My family habitually spoke to each other disrespectfully. As a child, it always hurt me. I thought my sister and I had learned to treat each other better. From my perspective, she spoke to me disrespectfully, then acted like nothing happened. I was appalled.

However, I had to step back to ask myself, "Is this my issue or hers?" I wanted to make it her issue, but I realized it was mine.

Going through this experience with my sister was difficult, but working through it eventually allowed me to see it was actually healing something deep inside of me. I realized I truly had no control over my sister's behavior. I got triggered and had an emotional reaction because this incident brought back to me those years as a child when my parents were fighting so often. I went right back to the old place of my wounding inside. It let me know my wounding was still there, waiting to be healed.

127

You must never forget you have complete power to control your response to what is happening to you and keep yourself safe. No one ever does anything to you as an adult. I let myself and my old trauma be triggered by her behavior and together we created drama—and I take full responsibility. Instead of allowing myself to be drawn into this drama, I needed to take care of my own little girl inside who was scared and upset. Instead, I had allowed our two wounded little girls to fight with each other.

Exploring Boundaries—Lesson 4: Boundary Protection and Empathy

Humans are empathetic beings. You sometimes don't even realize how much you are empathizing with other people's emotions or energy. You may sometimes be extra sad or angry when others around you are sad or angry. You may not mentally realize this is sometimes due to the other person's feelings. Some people can easily mirror and take on others' emotions.

Your brain is actually wired for empathy—it contains mirror neurons that are activated when you observe someone else. You are able to share others' feelings through the neurons in your brain. This is not a paranormal phenomenon; it is a biological fact that is now being studied. I believe some of you are much more sensitive in this area than others. You may have heard recent literature referring to this type of person as "highly sensitive."

Empathy overall is a very good thing unless you are over empathetic. This can leave you feeling drained and cause you to have excess feelings (i.e., anger and sadness). When this happens, you are not protecting your boundaries in a healthy way.

You can experience this in a variety of situations. One possibility is you may work with people who have a lot of stress, anger, or sadness. Sometimes without realizing it, you take on their feelings in your own body. In the therapy profession, this is actually called secondary trauma. You don't need to absorb the emotions of others;

you have enough of your own. You must learn to put a boundary around yourself. This is the same thing as setting physical boundaries with your loved ones, clients, or others in your life. The good news is you can learn how to set your boundaries, so you don't take on the energy of others. Understanding how to set your boundaries is very important to allow you to maintain your positive level of energy.

COACHING ACTION

The next technique can be used in the following situations:

1. Someone's behavior feels stressful to you.
2. Someone is angry in your presence.
3. You are in a situation where you feel anxiety.
4. You are in a situation where you have no idea what emotions others are feeling (e.g., plane, hotel, hospital).
5. You are in a stressful situation.
6. You will be entering a situation that will have a lot of pain and emotion (e.g., emergency professionals).
7. At any point in life.

With this technique you create the intention that you will not allow others' emotions to affect your energy. This technique allows you to stand strong in your power no matter the situation you are in.

1. You can be standing or sitting.
2. Take three deep breaths.
3. Think about letting go of anything you do not need. If you want, move your body, stretch to release any tension.
4. Close your eyes and bring your attention to the center of your body, deep inside of your body.
5. Take a deep breath.
6. Envision a huge bubble of peaceful, loving energy in front of you. It is swirling. You can step into the bubble

or bring it around you. Envision it encircling your body. Feel its energy; its protection and safety. It is your protection. It ensures you are not vulnerable to anything not in your best interest.

7. The bubble is around you; with your eyes still closed, follow its edges in your mind, making its outer edge very strong. Do this by rolling your eyes inside your head.

8. Take a deep breath and say the following: *Higher Power, I thank you for this protection. I thank you for allowing me to stand in my power and strength. I ask that you allow all good things to permeate this bubble and allow this bubble to guard me against anything not in my highest good. I know I am protected as I do my work in this world. I am powerful. I thank you.*

Exploring Boundaries—Lesson 5: The Ability to Say "No"

Sometimes we feel once we decide to do something, we cannot make another choice. This is not true. Oftentimes, you can show more integrity by choosing *not* to do things you have already taken on. This can be an act of setting healthy boundaries. One of my clients told me that due to her attention deficit disorder, she sometimes forgets what she has agreed to do and will take more things on than she can handle. This eventually moves her into a state of overwhelm, which is where she lives a lot of her life.

When we discussed that she can actually choose not to do things she has taken on, she realized she had so much more freedom. There may be consequences of not choosing to do something. However, when you compromise your integrity and freedom, the consequences are much greater. Also, remember it is not that you *can't* do it, but that you are *choosing* not to. This is a very big difference.

For example, maybe you said for the past year you were going to put up new curtains. You can decide to not hang the curtains, and just take it off your list (this also could be a committee you are on, a side job you said you would do, a relationship). Of course, we are all

adults and it goes without saying if we are going to break a commitment, to maintain our integrity, we will need to have all necessary
conversations with those we had commitments with to let them
know we will not be fulfilling that commitment. Once you have chosen not to hang the curtains, though, take note of how free you feel.

COACHING ACTION

What have you taken on in your life that does not serve you
well? Make a list of commitments. Assess if each serves you or if it is
something you should take off your list. Yes, **you** have that power.

List everything here, get it all out.

Project/Work/ Issue/ Relationship	Will I Complete or Not? (Yes or No)	By When?

Where else in your life do you need to say no to something or
someone?

Exploring Boundaries—Lesson 6: Boundaries and Unhealthy Behaviors

I recently worked with a client who is married to a man who
controls and manipulates her life. This was a pattern in her relationships. My client needed to look within herself. She needed to ask herself what story she was telling herself that allowed her to choose men
time and again who were verbally and physically abusive to her. What

allows her to accept this behavior and not set healthy boundaries? She is an attractive woman inside and out, but she has to be telling herself, for some reason, she does not deserve to be treated better.

The first time her boyfriend, now husband, said something rude or condescending to her, she chose to accept it, not respect herself, and move on, rather than set a boundary right then and tell him, "no more." When you respect yourself, others can respect you. When you set a boundary, sometimes the other person will listen and stop the negative behavior. Sometimes they won't stop the behavior and then you have a choice to make. Let's be clear, this is a choice. Yet, with people in your life who treat you badly, you may feel unable to stand up to them or make a healthy choice. You may feel you don't have the right.

My client told me she thought the situation would get better. "What is there to get better about someone mistreating you?" I asked. Again, it's about self-love. She needed to find the love of herself to be able to say no to any behavior not healthy for her. When you are confident in who you are and you have self-love, you no longer tolerate unhealthy behaviors.

I believe all things happen for a reason. She selected this man to work on this old untrue story she tells herself—for some reason she is not good enough to be treated respectfully. Yet, if she can break through this story by setting her boundaries and standing up for herself, this relationship will be worth it. Remember, relationships are our biggest teachers.

COACHING ACTION

If you find yourself caught in a similar situation, use these steps to help yourself get through it.

First, you must recognize when someone is not treating you well. You also may not be treating someone else well. You must be able to admit this behavior is unhealthy and violates your boundaries of self-love.

Think about what patterns you witnessed in your life (most likely as a child or young adult) that told you this behavior was acceptable in some way?

Take a deep breath, close your eyes, and ask yourself:

1. Why do I allow myself to be hurt or hurt others this way?
2. When I find myself in this pattern again, what do I need to do to STOP this pattern?
3. What new healthy pattern will I create?
4. What boundary do I need to set with this other person (or myself) to ensure this healthy pattern happens?

Once you have found your beauty and strength, you will not allow it to be covered up again so easily. You will fight for it. You will fight for your freedom. Healthy boundaries truly provide us with freedom. When you develop healthy boundaries, you will not allow others to trample and trespass your fences again. You also will not trample or trespass others' fences. Life will be much easier as a direct result of self-love.

Exploring Boundaries—Lesson 7: Developing Inner Strength and Love

You will only find the inner strength to set healthy boundaries from inner love. The deeper your self-love, the healthier your boundary choices will become. The inner strength you develop will allow you to make the choice that is right for you. When I was younger and in a difficult relationship, I often found myself going back to the person even when the relationship was not good. I did this because I did not have my inner strength or love developed. I did not love myself enough; therefore, I had not learned how to establish boundaries for what I would or would not tolerate. In my more recent relationships, I have been much stronger because I finally learned how to love and respect myself. I want the best for myself. I know I am worth it and I am important. You must love yourself enough to do the right thing for you. You are worth it.

My client who is in the abusive and controlling relationship has not yet realized her amazing inner beauty. This is something only she can do. You cannot get this from someone else. Simply being with someone else does not allow you to love yourself more. You are the only one who can take a stand and love you. Relationships reveal our weak spots and allow us to love ourselves more, if we choose.

Go ahead and take steps to get assistance in this process by contacting a coach or counselor. I know it is not easy; take baby steps. Know there are many others who can help you if you reach out and ask. Most importantly, if you catch yourself making excuses about why you can't do this, look at *why* you are making excuses.

COACHING ACTION

1. Close your eyes and take a deep breath.
2. Put your hand on your lower stomach area. Imagine you can see inside yourself.
3. Ask yourself: *What is my inner strength? At my core, what qualities make me strong?* Connect to your deep inner strength.
4. Listen to what you hear, or just connect with the feeling of strength.
5. Breathe into these qualities.
6. Say the following:
   I am strong
   I am _____
   (insert all qualities or just breathe into the strong feeling you have),
7. See or simply feel this strength deep, deep, deep within you. Breathe into this feeling with five deep breaths. Say to yourself: *I am strong.*
8. Practice connecting daily to your deep inner strength.

Boundary Affirmation

*Please provide me with the inner strength and love to make choices and
set boundaries that support the beautiful person I am.*

Exploring Boundaries—Lesson 8: Healing Through Safety

SHARING MY STORY
Cultivating My Own Safety

As I journeyed closer to finishing this book, some big things
surfaced for me. Of course they would. I created a profound title and
intention talking about successful partnerships and self-love. When
you intend something, a Higher Power responds. And that they did.

My husband has a habit of shutting me out when he is frustrated with something I have done. At one point, he hung up on me
and shut me out for four days while he was working in Norway.
Those days challenged me to my core because I was not sure where
our relationship was going, as he would not talk to me about that.

The interesting fact is before I married my husband, a very
intuitive massage therapist said to me, "You know he is not going to
make you feel safe." I said, "Yes I know." I knew it was about me
feeling safe and not about him making me feel safe.

During the time when he was shutting me out, I would wake
up with anxiety in the middle of the night. During the last night of
his boycott, I woke up with such fear in my stomach and I asked the
angels to assist me in healing. They did. The coaching action below is
the meditation the angels gave me to help heal my safety issue.

After doing the meditation, I got up the next morning and
took care of me by getting a massage. As I drove, I thought, "No
matter what, I will be okay now that I know deep inside I am safe."
This situation brought me to the next level of ascension here on this
planet. There is something so crucial about knowing you are safe.

There is also something so valuable about the partners we choose to assist us in this healing. Amazingly, later that day, he contacted me.

What I learned from this is that safety is the most basic need we have and if for any reason we did not feel safe as a child, we must learn to cultivate this in ourselves in order to feel joy, love, and peace. Safety is the foundation for creating a magical life. We often look for safety and security from homes, religion, and others in our lives. We are the only ones who can provide this to ourselves. When we stop needing this from others, including partners and children, our lives will be much happier and fulfilled.

COACHING ACTION

1. Take your hands and put them on your stomach. Slowly move them back and forth above your navel.
2. Breathe slowly and take three deep breaths.
3. Say to yourself: *"I am safe."* As you continue the back and forth motion, you release any old fears about your safety.
4. As you are breathing, envision and feel a loving, kind, empathetic, patient, and calm mother energy. Feel this energy assisting you and being there for you.
5. Now, begin to see a web of safety being spun around you, like a beautiful cocoon. You are spinning it like a caterpillar. You are feeling loving mother energy infusing into the web as you do this. Breathe into this.
6. See the web and bring safety in through your hands.
7. Say to yourself five times: *"I am safe."* Then, change it to: *"You are safe."* This statement comes from that ever-present mother energy. The mother energy is coming from you. See yourself giving that loving energy of safety to yourself.
8. Continue to do this for a few minutes.
9. Do this every day this week. As you drive, place your hand on your stomach at any time and say: *"You are safe."*

Each morning for a couple minutes, close your eyes and feel this safe cocoon building around you. This is a process. It will immediately begin to create change. To sustain it and build your sense of true safety you must keep letting your body know this is the truth.

Exploring Boundaries—Lesson 9: Building a Circle of Trust

Building what I call the circle of trust in your relationships is critical. This is one of the most important things we can do to establish healthy relationships. All we really want as humans is to feel safe and secure. Trust lies at the foundation of all healthy relationships. When we feel safe and secure with others, we can trust them. Trust ensures that you create successful relationships at home and work.

Examples of how we build trust with others are:
- Praising others.
- Being patient.
- Being honest and keeping your word.
- Including others in your life.
- Setting your boundaries with others.

When you treat others this way, it helps them feel safe and trust you. When they trust you they can love you (if that is the relationship you have) or respect you.

COACHING ACTION

Take a moment and assess how you are doing at helping others feel safe and secure. To assess how you are doing at building a circle of trust in your life, complete the following:

Step 1:   Close your eyes. Envision you are standing in a big circle—a circle of trust. In the circle is everything that makes you feel safe and secure. Open your arms, palms face up, and breathe into this feeling.

Step 2:   Feel the safety and security this circle provides for you (this womb space you are creating for yourself).

Step 3:   Say to yourself: *I choose to stay in this safe space in my life, I can access this safe space at any time.*

Step 4:   Take a moment to review your current relationships (personal and professional). Ask yourself: *What do I need to do to strengthen this circle of trust in my relationships so others feel safe and secure with me?*

Step 5:   You can now envision each person in your life in front of you and you can ask them these questions:

1. What have I done to make you feel unsafe and insecure in our relationship?
2. What can I do to make you feel safer and more secure in our relationship?

Ask yourself now:

1. What can I do to build my trust with myself so I know I can make healthy choices in my relationships?
2. How is setting boundaries related to me accomplishing my future goal of successful relationships in life?

Summary

Healthy boundaries equal healthy relationships. Remember, boundaries are key to being able to accomplish what you want to in this life. With healthy boundaries, you have the foundation to connect deeply with others in a loving, nourishing way. Then you can create balanced, loving, respectful, and supportive relationships.

Healing Yourself Physically, Emotionally, and Spiritually

The journey of self-love is a process of healing all of you; mind, body, and spirit. In our society, healing usually means going to see a doctor. We have been conditioned to think that to get better emotionally or physically, we must see someone who will give us a quick fix, something to stop the problem. Covering up a symptom, however, often does not allow us to look at what the deeper issue may be. It is time for all of us to be open to alternative methods of health and well-being as we embark upon the journey of self-love.

I have come to understand it is very often a combination of modalities—alternative methods as well as medical interventions (drugs, surgery, etc.) that can best assist us. No matter what your choice is, you must truly want to heal for the method to assist you. You must believe you can get better, no matter what illness it may be. You must participate emotionally in your own process. There are many paths that lead us to freedom during this journey.

Think of any medical challenge you're experiencing as your body expressing that it's out of balance. Then, be open to the many ways, including holistic options, to assist your body to be in harmony and balance. When you are in balance, you thrive. I have read so many stories of women who were told by the medical professionals they could not have children, but they had a child naturally after they took the time to get their body and life in balance.

Health issues are opportunities for you to attend to yourself on a deeper emotional level. When you unconsciously say, "Something is wrong with my body and the doctor must fix it," you are missing a larger piece of the puzzle. Even conventional physicians agree, you need to look at the emotional side of your mental or physical issue.

Many people miss the huge gift of illness if they choose not to look at the emotional side. For example, past emotional pain, such as unresolved anger, can cause physical pain or imbalance in your body. Past emotional pain can also result in carrying around limiting beliefs. All of these things can block you from true health. Sometimes you have no idea these old beliefs exist.

The good news is many alternative methods give you the ability to create your own wellness through uncovering and releasing old beliefs and patterns that can be limiting you from achieving your full potential.

You will benefit immensely if you stay open to the many different possibilities you have access to during this journey of self-love. You will be transforming on an emotional, physical, and spiritual level as you deepen your self-love. The processes of emotional and physical well-being are so connected, they are almost impossible to truly separate.

Keep in mind that when you heal on an emotional level, you also transform your body on a physical level.

Healing Yourself—Lesson 1: Using Your Intuition as Your Guide

Intuition is an integral part of participating in your healing process. It allows you to discern what is right for you and what you should do next. If you take the time to listen to your heart and soul, you can assist in healing yourself. Your intuition can guide you to live your most desired life.

Over time, my intuition has become stronger, just like any skill I practice. As you focus on developing your intuition, you must trust and believe you have the ability just to "know." You have it; you just don't always take the time to be quiet and listen to it. It is right there waiting for you. Intuition is an inner feeling. It is your guide, your personal GPS. You may also want to call on your Higher Power to help guide you in what is right for you as you access your intuition.

I feel the source of my intuition is at my core, or directly inside my navel, which makes sense to me because this area is your first connection to life via the umbilical cord. Intuition is when you "tune into" yourself and your life. Most of the time, you know what to do, but you don't take the time to slow down and listen to yourself.

Learning to listen to yourself through your intuition is a key component of this book. The lessons in this book are designed to provide you with opportunities to listen more deeply to yourself. Once you have completed this book, you will be able to continue to use your intuition. It is my hope you will use your intuition to know the next best thing to do to take care of you for the rest of your life.

The next time you want to consult with a medical professional or another care provider, I challenge you to consult yourself first. Of course, if you are experiencing a medical emergency, I always advise seeking the proper medical care first and foremost. However, in a non-emergency, you may find the answers lie within. In the model of coaching in which I was trained, I do not provide answers to my clients. I am simply a catalyst to assist them to uncover their greatness through the use of their intuition, which includes health issues. I ask deep questions that come from my intuition to bring out their intuition and inner knowing. This creates the space for them to heal and move forward in their lives. Working with your own intuition is a crucial aspect of deepening your self-love. No one else knows what is best for you like you do. Good health in all areas of your body will promote healing and access to self-love.

SHARING MY STORY
Listening and Healing My Body

I was forty-two-years-old working with a fertility doctor. I also was using other natural methods to create a healthy body. The doctor told my husband and me that we most likely needed in vitro fertilization, IVF, and we could try an intrauterine insemination IUI,. Before this, they give you fertility drugs to stimulate your eggs. I had many ultrasounds and once I had taken the fertility drug, they did an ultrasound to see if my eggs were the right size.

The eggs were the right size. I believe they would have been right with or without the drug, but now they saw something strange on the ultrasound. I had to go through a very painful procedure where they looked at my uterus to see what it was. They also stopped the process of the IUI at this point, because they could not determine what the spot on my uterus was. It turned out to be a polyp.

The doctor recommended surgery, which I did set up. But I decided first to do a lot of reading on this and found out that a polyp was not a threat to my life, but was a concern, although not a huge one, if I tried to get pregnant. The doctors would not proceed with IVF without doing the procedure, however.

Something did not feel right. I worked with my coach and I decided to take my power back and not have the surgery. That saved me $2,000 and I felt intuitively it was the right thing to do. I also intuitively felt the fertility drug had possibly caused the growth. The doctors never mentioned anything about that. I started doing Mayan massage and essential oils. I continued my green smoothies and fertility tea. When I went back to the doctor five-months later, I made sure to look at the ultrasound with the nurse. We saw nothing. When I met with the doctor, he said the polyp needed to be removed before he could proceed with any procedures. I informed him I was sure it was gone. He did an ultrasound himself, for free even, and wow, it was gone. He was amazed.

Always listen to yourself. I saved myself an operation I did not need and $2,000 I did not need to spend. More importantly, I took back my power around my fertility journey. I felt empowered versus the disempowerment I felt from someone telling me what I *had* to do.

Intuition is a part of who you are, and we all have it. Your role in accessing your intuition is to allow yourself to be open to it. Have you ever felt like you just knew something? That is intuition. Let's take the time to slow down and connect to your intuition with the following exercise. Once you begin to listen to yourself and your own wisdom, you'll be amazed at what you will hear.

COACHING ACTION

Find a quiet place and prepare to spend some time asking yourself these questions and listening to the answers.

1. Ask yourself:
   - *Do I deserve to be listened to?*
   - *How can I better listen to myself?*
   - *How can I slow down?*
2. Say aloud, *I trust I have intuition. I know I can guide my own life at a deeper level. I don't have to go to others for any of my answers. I have all the answers I need.*
3. Take a deep breath and continue to focus on slow, deep breaths for at least a minute. Connect to yourself. Connect to your core—your belly button area.
4. Envision a table in front of you. Put any current question or issue in your life you are dealing with on the table. Ask the question out loud or in your mind and notice what you hear or see. If you don't see or hear anything at first, say aloud, *I know the answer to this.* Be patient as you listen and breathe.
5. Continue this process with as many questions as you want concerning what is going on in your life. With practice, this

exercise will allow you to sharpen your ability to listen to the answers you already have within yourself.

Healing Yourself—Lesson 2: Alternative Modalities—Healing Body, Mind, and Spirit

The healing process cannot be rushed. At times, you will feel instant benefits from a healing method you choose, and at other times, you will wonder if a particular modality is working. Know if you are led to something, it will assist you on some level. You cannot always mentally understand the level of healing that occurs. Instead, trust that each training, seminar, or healer provides something valuable for you.

Of course, you need to use your judgment and if something does not feel right, you can choose not to partake in that particular form of healing. In other words, listen to your body and your intuition. You are your ultimate guide. Never give away your power to anyone, alternative healing methods, or the medical community.

COACHING ACTION

There are countless alternative healing options. During my journey of self-love, I've personally experienced each of the following alternative healing options I am going to share with you below. Most of these options assisted me to heal emotional pain. Some of them assisted me with physical pain. Emotional and physical pain are so interconnected when you heal one, you typically heal the other.

In the information below, I've provided what each particular method healed for me or how it touched my life. The definitions are not formal definitions because you can research to get that anywhere.

Some of the methods will be new to you and may even seem strange. My coaching message is to keep an open mind to what could truly assist you in living your healthiest life.

1. Read through the following healing modalities.
2. If any of these intrigue you, put a star by them and research additional information and practitioners in your area in order to decide if it is a fit for you.

Acupuncture:

At points in my life, acupuncture helped me lower my stress and anxiety when I felt overwhelmed by life. It also helped me balance and increase my energy level when I was working too hard. Acupuncture helped move the energy in my body and assisted me in being calmer. I have also used it to relieve pain in my body.

Breath Work:

I first experienced breath work many years ago. I worked with a practitioner who had me breathe deeply as I lay on a massage table fully clothed. He witnessed my breathing process. He sat with me the entire time. I knew I was safe, even though I did not feel very comfortable breathing so deeply (a strange, but true phenomenon). A lot of old emotions and fears arose, which I was able to release. He taught me to breathe more deeply to release these old feelings.

Another time in my life, when I was grieving the end of a relationship, I went to a group meditation and breathing session. In this session, the instructor had us breathing deeply and slowly while he played special music. What arose from my body was some very old subconscious grief from when I was four years old and my aunt had a miscarriage of her pregnancy at seven months. She was living with my family at the time and we shared a room. I thought of her unborn baby as my new sibling. When my aunt left one evening and did not return with a baby, I had no method of processing my grief. I truly felt the baby simply left me. I had learned from my other healing experiences that this loss was an issue for me, but I had never been able to cry and release the old subconscious grief until this meditation.

Coaching:

Coaching has played a pivotal role in allowing me to realize my true strength and accept the fact that I deserve to create the life of my dreams. My coaches act as reflectors for me, so I can see the big picture of my life more clearly. Coaching provided me with innumerable gifts. Working with my first coach fifteen years ago I uncovered my truth that I am a coach at heart. Becoming a coach has been one of the best decisions I have ever made. Every coach is different, and I do recommend a coach who has been officially trained in a certified coach training program.

Cranial Sacral:

This healing modality has rave reviews by many. It assists with emotional release and rebalancing of the body. The cranial sacral technique is said to rebalance the bones of your cranium. The practitioner places their hands on the back of your head while you are lying on a massage table. Then, they do their magic while working with the bones of your skull. I feel calm and balanced afterward. I also did this after a mild concussion, and my sense was it was very helpful to rebalance my nervous system.

EFT or Emotional Freedom Technique:

In some instances, using this technique of tapping on certain points of my body helped me process and feel calmer after a relationship ended. It also has helped me return quickly to my balanced center and is easy to do in any situation. It helps you connect back to your body.

EMDR—Eye Movement Desensitization and Reprogramming:

Through re-experiencing traumatic events in a safe environment, EMDR helped me see patterns running my life. EMDR helps you become aware of and release old patterns and anxiety.

Healing Touch/Hands-On Healing:

Healing touch works at an energetic/body level. It helps me relax and let go. I feel lighter and freer after a session. It can also heal some of our old attachment wounds by giving us the peace of loving connection that is hard to explain. It also assists when people are sick to give them peace, especially if they are in hospice or will be passing soon. The practitioner may or may not put their hands on you. They work with your energy field to create positive energy shifts for you. The experiences I shared here are from my own experiences as a healing touch practitioner and my experience receiving healing touch.

Hypnotherapy:

Hypnotherapy feels like a deep level of relaxation, so the body can do its own healing. I have been able to release old feelings and emotions from my body. When I am releasing old stuff in the session, my body actually feels hot, which is a sign to me that old energy is moving through my cells. I have been able to release old issues with my parents at a more subconscious level. It has also allowed me to lower my level of anxiety. You are in complete control of your actions, just very relaxed, so you can process on a different level.

Homeopathy:

Homeopathy is based on the idea that "like cures like"—a substance, the remedy, taken in small amounts will cure the same symptoms it causes if it was taken in large amounts. I did homeopathy very early in my journey, and I believe it was helpful. It allowed me to release some old emotion. After taking my remedy, I remember part of my face turning bright red, and I then remembered I used to be slapped by one of my parents in that exact spot. The remedy, usually derived from a plant or mineral, is a minute dose of what the practitioner feels you may need to heal once they do your intake. I believe the remedy that I took was releasing that old pain and energy. It activated something inside of me and brought it to the surface, so I could heal at a deeper level.

Kirtan:

This is singing in Sanskrit or words you usually do not know. The words are beautiful mantras. Not knowing what the words mean is said to be positive because if our minds know the words we put meaning to the words. Not knowing the words allows us to experience the positive vibration of the words only. Whatever it is, it uplifts my spirit and energy. They say the words have universal resonance, even though we have no idea what we are saying. I always feel lighter and happier after Kirtan.

Massage:

For me, massage is quite relaxing. I get a massage when I need to take care of myself. I have used it when I felt down or alone because it always helps me feel nurtured and cared for. I also use it when my body is feeling physical pain to release tension. I believe it has also assisted me in releasing the old emotional pain that has manifested as physical pain in my body. It can also assist you in accepting healthy and safe positive touch if that is important to you.

Meditation (Guided):

Guided meditation brings a level of calm and peace. For my own healing, I wrote my own meditations. They came to me during a time of deep healing after moving to Boulder, Colorado. They helped me love myself and heal at a very deep, cellular level. They have also assisted in healing my body. They allowed me to bring more abundance into my life. I bought my dream home in the mountains not long after writing them. My meditation CDs are, *The Healing Journey Within: Meditations for Abundance and Love: Volume I Deserving* (http://amzn.to/2h82t8y) and *The Healing Journey Within: Meditations for Abundance and Love: Volume II Manifesting* (http://amzn.to/2h0aVua). Many who have completed my CDs report they are one of the most peaceful and nurturing things they have done for themselves and their self-love. For beginning meditators or corporate leaders, I always recommend Jon Kabat-Zinn's guided meditations.

Music/Mantras:

Through my yoga teacher training in Kundalini yoga (which includes movement, breathing techniques, meditation, and mantras), I was exposed to many spiritual singers, such as Snatum Kaur, as well as many mantras and meditations for healing. The words to these beautiful songs are uplifting and resonate love. This music helped to keep me grounded and positive.

Some mantras in Sanskrit are very powerful, such as Om Nama Shivaya and the Gayatri Mantra. I once recited the Gayatri Mantra 108 times for thirty days. This was a very healing experience for me that helped me quiet my mind. I've also learned that listening to consciousness-raising or classical music clears my mind.

Reiki:

Reiki, a form of energy healing, helps me feel calm and peaceful. It takes me to a deep level of relaxation. It is also a method of stress reduction that promotes healing of the body, mind, and spirit.

Soul Retrieval:

I worked with a Native American man who worked with his spirit guides to take me back through any challenging times in my life. Most importantly, we explored a time when I was hit by a car. This man explained sometimes our souls get stuck at these events, and we play out this stuckness in our current lives. He said the vibrant young girl I was when the accident happened—that part of my soul—was still at the crash site. He helped me bring her back and know it was safe to live and love fully in the world. He also assured me that as a child I was always kept safe by Grandmother Moon (a feminine leader in Native traditions who watches over the children of the earth), which was very reassuring to me.

Sound Healing:

Sound healing is very relaxing and has allowed me to do some wonderful healing. The instruments resonate with and balance my body. One person plays an instrument, such as singing bowls, a gong, or a didgeridoo (the world's oldest wind instrument that is blown into to create a deep primal sound), as the participants lie down and relax. I met a special friend at a music festival, and intuitively I asked him if I could lie down and he could play his double didgeridoo over me. It felt extremely grounding and nurturing.

Sweat Lodge:

This Native American tradition has been powerful in my life. A proper sweat lodge is an igloo-looking structure made of willow branches and natural fiber blankets. Inside the lodge, in the middle of the dirt floor, is a divot/hole in the ground, lower than the rest of the lodge. A fire burns for many hours outside. In this outside fire (under the wood), there are many rocks that get very hot. When the rocks are hot enough, everyone goes inside the lodge and sits in a circle on the ground. The rocks are then brought inside the lodge into the hole in the ground. Water is poured on the rocks, creating a very hot and steamy atmosphere. There is a lot of sweating. The chants recited are beautiful, and the experience is very cleansing, releasing, and healing for me. The sweat lodge feels like a mother's womb; there is solace and peace for me when I am there in the darkness and breathing in the heat. It is also liberating when I come out of the womb (which is the feeling the dark sweat lodge creates) into the light. After moving to Colorado, I had the honor to assist in building a sweat lodge; it was a sacred experience.

Yoga:

I sometimes say yoga saved my life. My mat has been my second home over the last fifteen years. When I traveled solo to Guatemala, I happened to take a Kundalini yoga class (which I knew nothing about at the time). It was so powerful for me in releasing old emotions I knew I wanted to be a teacher. I am now a trained Kundalini yoga teacher. I later learned from Gurmukh that Kundalini is called the yoga of self-love. Yoga brings me home to me.

Be selective about your yoga teacher. Ensure they teach from their heart and bring a peaceful calm to the yoga class. For yoga to be true yoga some form of meditation should exist in the class. The most important part is called Shavasana. It is the time—at least five minutes at the end of the class—when you lie down, breathe, relax, and integrate what you learned. If you jump right up and run back to life, you miss the true benefit of yoga because this quiet time is when you truly heal.

Yoga Nidra:

When I was ill and had pain in movement (prior to being dairy and gluten-free and taking probiotics) I found Yoga Nidra (yogic sleep which is a state of consciousness between waking and sleeping). It is similar to guided meditation. My experience was a very deep relaxation, and afterward, I felt as though I'd had a deep rest. Yoga Nidra is a very powerful for allowing you to relax deeply and heal.

Did any of these methods seem interesting, spark something in you, or bring up emotion? If yes, I urge you to delve further to see if any of these may be one of the healing modalities to assist you.

To be clear, there are many more modalities you can use to facilitate your own healing. These are just the ones I have used on my journey. If you know there is something specific you want to heal, ask your Higher Power to guide you in finding the best method for your healing. When you ask, you shall receive.

Healing Yourself—Lesson 3: Healing Techniques

As you probably realize, meditations have been very important to me in creating a deeper self-love. Because of their importance, I am including two of the most important techniques I created and have used for healing. I share them with the hope they will be helpful to you as well. Use these meditations whenever you need them. You may also revise them in any way that feels right to you.

151

COACHING ACTION

To be fully present in life, it is important to make sure you are connected with the Earth. You can provide this calm connection to Mother Earth for yourself without having to be out in nature.

Use this Grounding to Love technique for the following:
- Before an important meeting or conversation to calm yourself and help you think clearly
- To calm any type of anxiety
- After you have been with a stressful or angry person
- If you really want to focus or be present
- To let go of negative thoughts

To perform this technique on yourself, do the following:

1. You can be seated or standing.
2. Put both of your feet flat on the ground with your arms by your sides or in your lap.
3. Close your eyes and take three deep breaths.
4. Envision a beautiful gold cord attached to your left foot.
5. Envision the cord dropping down into the Earth, to the center of the Earth, where there is a beautiful pink and white heart stone or rose quartz crystal. This is the Earth's heart center of love.
6. See the cord from your left foot wrapping around the beautiful rose quartz at the center of the Earth.
7. Now envision the other end of the golden cord coming up and connecting to the bottom of your right foot.
8. This cord is your anchor, pulling you into the loving energy of Mother Earth.
9. Take three deep breaths and envision the cord pulling you strongly down into the Earth's heart space. Feel it tugging you snugly to the Earth.

10. Feel how good it is to be calm in your body. This is what we call being "grounded" because you are solidly feeling your connection to the ground, the Earth. This is the deep connection Native Americans speak of, the Mother Earth connection of deep love and gratitude.

11. Take five deep breaths to anchor this feeling in your body. With each breath, say something you need to hear, like, "I am beautiful." Feel yourself solidly connect to the Earth. You will now move into the day more present and connected with yourself and your center.

COACHING ACTION

This Rebalancing and Calming Healing Technique is important for bringing you back into balance after an incident or experience has left you feeling out of balance. This technique will allow you to clear any unwanted energy from the space around you that may impact your ability to be calm and peaceful.

You may benefit from the Rebalancing and Calming Healing Technique if you are experiencing or have experienced the following:

- An angry interaction with someone
- A difficult interaction with someone that leaves you feeling upset
- An overall feeling of sadness
- A feeling of overwhelm
- Witnessing the anger or extreme sadness of someone else
- Working with populations that are extremely sad, hurt, depressed, or angry (all therapists should do this after each day)

To perform hands-on self-healing, please do the following:

1. Sit or stand.
2. Close your eyes and take three deep breaths.
3. With your eyes closed, focus inward.
4. Think of the word "release" in your mind.
5. Set the intention to release anything you do not need and say to yourself, *I release anything I do not need.*
6. You can open your eyes if you want at this point.
7. Hold both arms straight up above you, turn both palms down, and push them outward.
8. Move your arms slowly out from your body and down just a bit, as if you were pushing anything you do not need out into space. I think of pushing snow off evergreen tree branches that are sloped downward. Push anything you don't need out of your space. Start near your body, and push your hands outward, symbolizing releasing old stuff.
9. As you do this, think to yourself, *I release anything I do not need.* You can also think of a specific thing you want to release, such as anxiety, sadness, or anger.
10. At the end of this movement, flick your fingers outward in a motion of releasing anything your hands are now holding. You are letting go of anything you do not need.
11. Breathe deeply as you do this.
12. Bring your arms back up above your head; bring your hands down about three to four inches (they will still be above your head) and do this practice again.
13. Move all the way down your body three to four inches at a time until you reach your feet, doing this same sweeping motion seven to ten times. You never actually need to touch your body.
14. You have now released the unneeded energy that was surrounding you. This energy could have come from

numerous places; just know now it has dissipated. Intend that it goes to the positive light.

15. Take two deep breaths.

16. Begin again with your arms stretched out above your head, and think of a positive word you would like to bring into your energy. It could be peace, love, calm, or whatever you want.

17. Repeat the process, but as you move your arms outward, think the word in your mind. This time, visualize putting that energy of peace or calm into your energy field.

18. Complete by saying the following, *I thank you, Higher Power, for your guidance and healing today. Thank you for allowing me to heal myself, which is the ultimate form of healing for me.*

Summary

Begin now to regularly ask your intuition for guidance and listen to it. You can initially ask it very simple questions and then progress to bigger questions. Your body, mind, and spirit are one-hundred percent connected. Caring for one of these will positively impact the others. I promise you, as you take time and energy to heal your body, mind, and spirit, you will heal your life.

ACCEPT NATURAL HEALING METHODS AS SELF-LOVE CURES

On so many levels, you are your own best healer and there are many ways in which you can facilitate your own healing.

All of the natural methods I share in this chapter have allowed me to find a deeper love within, providing me with over fifty percent of my self-love growth. These methods play a huge role in my life and have been crucial to my success on this self-love journey—giving me a higher quality of life and providing beautiful and, often unexpected, gifts along the way.

You have access to countless resources, many of which are free, to assist you in loving yourself deeper. There is not one single miracle cure, but rather a combination. You and you alone will find out which methods will best assist you in healing naturally, so you can find true love within. You must trust yourself and your intuition to guide you.

The best news is you can do any of these methods any time, on your own. Including natural methods in your life is a key to your success in achieving sustainable self-love. I share the best methods I have found below.

Natural Healing Method 1: Nature

Nature is the easiest to access, most natural, loving, and best healer in the world. Children who grow up in very difficult environments—often those that include abuse and violence—report that being outdoors provides a solace for them. I believe these children instinctively seek out the comfort of nature in order to nurture their souls. I know nature was one of my greatest healers as a child and as I have traveled solo. As adults, it is important to continue spending time outside in order to continuously recharge and heal.

We each may have different methods for healing in nature, but I believe there is no better medicine than the Earth around us. I say this as I sit writing near Boulder Creek on a gorgeous day in Colorado. I hear the calm gurgle of the creek as it flows by, I feel the hello of the soft breeze on my neck, and I see the amazing strength, beauty, and power of the mountains in the distance. The mountains have always been nurturing for me, just as the water is calming.

When I was a runner, I always sought out places where I could run near water. I ran with the peace of the water enveloping my body, mind, and soul with each step. I also envisioned the water absorbing all my anxiety and stress. Hiking in nature is healing for me as well. When I hike, I feel grounded, peaceful, and calm.

As I sit and watch the babbling brook, I feel nature speaking to me. I always listen for its messages. It tells me I am loved. I am nurtured by Mother Earth and nature. Isn't it interesting how nature and nurture are such similar words?

Spending time in nature can also mean going on a wonderful vacation and spending as much time as possible outdoors. However, it's not necessary to leave home—just go outside wherever you are, as often as you can. When you are outside, take the time to connect with the nature around you.

As I sit here by the creek, small children are chasing each other, laughing and enjoying the beautiful outdoors. Their eyes are wide; they are clearly enthralled by the scampering squirrels, the rustling leaves, and the glistening water.

If you find you are not amazed and soothed by nature as an adult, it may be you were not exposed to it much when you were a child. Now is the time to begin exploring nature; it's never too late.

COACHING ACTION

1. The next chance you get, go outdoors and look at nature with the eyes of a child. Look up at the blue sky, feel the loving warm energy of the sun, smile, open your arms wide, and breathe. It will immediately change your outlook and the way you feel inside. Be open to seeing what nature wants to teach you. Be curious. Find your child inside.

2. To be grounded and to feel calm, I recommend lying on your back on the grass or ground for a few minutes. Envision being connected to the divine Mother Earth. She is always there for you. She takes care of you whenever you need it.

Natural Healing Method 2: Nutrition

Nutrition is essential to mental and physical healing. The right foods can heal your body. I read every product label. If it has many ingredients or I cannot pronounce them, I do not purchase the product. Some food companies will do anything to increase profits, often compromising our animals, our crops, and our overall food quality. To ensure you have the best quality food, do not eat highly processed foods. Buy local and organic whenever possible.

SHARING MY STORY
Healing Myself through Food

At age thirty-nine, after enjoying good overall health most of my life, I was sick with arthritic and chronic-fatigue symptoms. I had a constant low-grade fever. I sought advice from many traditional doctors. The last one I saw told me, "We sometimes never find the cure for these things."

Was he joking? I honestly could not believe he was saying that to me. That doctor made me so angry and I set out on a quest to heal myself.

I began reading everything I could on the symptoms I had and watched a PBS special on arthritis pain. The data I gathered was telling me this was an issue stemming from my gut and my immune system, which the gut is a huge part of. I removed dairy and gluten from my diet. This initially meant all bread and anything containing wheat on the label. I also took a probiotic supplement every day, per Brenda Watson's suggestion on the PBS special. I healed myself through these nutritional changes. It felt like a miracle, but it was a combination of nutrition and me listening to my body.

I received an unexpected benefit when I eliminated gluten; I mentally felt happier. I no longer experienced the up and down mood swings. This was unexpected at the time because I had eliminated gluten purely for the physical pain. I have since learned that gluten intolerance can be related to mental health. Your gut, where gluten can cause issues, is directly related to your brain. If you are experiencing any emotional or physical pain of any kind, my advice would be to remove gluten from your diet and see how you feel.

Another crucial piece for me has been limiting my sugar intake. If I have an addiction in life, it is sugar. Sugar is not our friend—in fact; you can increase your quality of life by eliminating sugar at any age. Now in my early forties, with my hormones changing, sugar immensely affects my moods and energy level. I can get angry easily after I eat sugar and my blood sugar spikes. About thirty minutes later I get tired. It is not worth it to me to eat much sugar any longer. I value my relationship with my husband more than sugar. I was able to eliminate night sweats and regulate my hormones on my own by cutting sugar out of my diet. I had previously been prescribed bio-identical hormones, which I have since stopped taking. The hormone doctor did not even ask about my diet, he just put me on medication. For some women, eliminating sugar is an important step in ensuring their hormones are more balanced, especially for fertility and menopausal reasons.

I do not eat any form of sugar unless it is from pure sources such as honey or maple syrup, and even then, only in small amounts.

I also eat a limited amount of fruit, mostly berries, but consume no fruit juices. However, I feel the best when I completely eliminate sugar of any kind (with the exception of some fruit). I can now put in my recipes one-third of the sugar others use and it still feels like too much. Everybody is different, so you must decide what changes in your diet will be ultimately best for your body. As always consult your health practitioner regarding what is best for you.

The bottom line is nutrition is crucial for your optimal health. It is a foundational piece to your success on this journey of healthy relationships and self-love. I ask you to consider the impact nutrition may be having on any issue in your life.

COACHING ACTION

Close your eyes, take three deep breaths, ask your body the following questions, sit quietly and listen for the answers:

What do I need to eat less of to increase my health?
What do I need to drink less of to increase my health?
What do I need to eat more of to increase my health?
What do I need to drink more of to increase my health?
What one step will I commit to doing to improve my health through nutrition?

Natural Healing Method 3: Solo Travel/Time

Traveling solo has been one of the most healing gifts I have given myself on this journey of self-love. It has also been one of the most fun gifts. I have been to many Third World countries and I have volunteered with many children. I have met so many beautiful people who are also on their journey. Solo travel is magical to me. It can feel addicting once you get started. Exploring new places is so exciting. I usually never have a plan when I arrive in a country; I just go and see where the wind takes me.

I began to travel solo in my thirties when my friends were getting married and having children. I wanted my own family, but in the absence of it, solo travel made me happy. It was something I looked forward to and since I worked for myself, I was often able to take two or three weeks off at a time.

The lessons you receive while traveling are invaluable. I learned some people have fewer physical possessions than we do in the U.S.; however, they were actually happier and more fulfilled. I learned not to judge anyone else's situation. I remember a man carrying what looked like a ton of bricks on his head in Guatemala. As he walked by, he flashed me the happiest smile I have ever seen.

Through solo travel, you realize your own strength and courage. You have a lot of time to connect with yourself. You weather many storms, both literal and figurative, all on your own. My favorite trips have been to Guatemala, India, Peru, and Thailand. These were my four major solo trips. I fully recommend scheduling a solo trip, even if for only a day or weekend. You will be amazed at what you find out about yourself and the world around you.

COACHING ACTION

First, let's dream a bit. Close your eyes (lie down if possible) and ask yourself: *If I could go anywhere right now, where would that be?*

Look at your life and current schedule. Depending on your situation, can you:

1. Take an evening for you?
2. Take a day for you?
3. Take a weekend away for you?
4. Take a week away just for you?
5. Take three weeks?

Be brave, you can do more than you think is possible. I know this. What would be outside your comfort zone? Whichever one you chose, I challenge you to do the next level. What could be possible in your life if you take this step just for you? What can you commit to right now? What do you need to do to make this happen?

Natural Healing Method 4: Letting Go

Letting go is one of the first steps in your healing process. Holding onto old junk blocks your growth. If you build a new foundation on the old junk, you will not create a new solid and secure foundation. We all have stuff we can release. To give yourself room to heal, begin with letting go. You will then have a clearer foundation from which to grow. This exercise allows you to excavate the old junk you may be storing in your body.

COACHING ACTION

You are the most important aspect of this process. You and only you can choose to let go of old stuff and heal your past. You can use a form (a form you may create yourself) of the following exercise at any time in your life to assist you in letting go.

1. Close your eyes and take two, deep breaths. Relax your body. Feel your body connecting to your chair or wherever you are. Allow all parts of your body to relax.
2. Ask yourself: *What is it I no longer need in my life?*
3. Say out loud: *Let go*, and hold an imaginary shovel in your hand. Make the motion as if you are scooping what you don't need out of your body. Envision what you no longer need in your life as dirt leaving your body in this shovel. You don't even have to know what it is. Let it go; it no longer serves you. Breathe.
4. Keep doing this action of digging out the junk and see what shows up. Relax into your body. Notice where you

are digging from. Are there any old fears you have that you know you need to clear out? Breathe.

5. Say out loud: *I release all I don't need to create my most beautiful life,* as you keep the small digging motion. Breathe. Continue digging for as long as it feels right.

6. Put the shovel down and say the following to yourself: *Higher Power, please reach your hand deep into my soul and clear away all nonessential debris. Allow me to release anything I do not need at this time to the Earth of the universe, so it may be transformed and used for good in the world. Thank you for your many blessings. Thank you for your infinite strength and wisdom.*

7. Relax your body. Let go. Breathe.

8. Now, envision something you want to bring into your life. See this in your life in whatever way you want it. Feel the emotion you will feel when you have this in your life. Breathe deeply into this.

Natural Healing Method 5: Meditation

Meditation is a wonderful process of connecting to yourself. This is one of the easiest, most cost-effective ways to return to optimal health. In our society today, we are so involved in "doing" versus "being." I work with a client who is a very high performer. He is all about accomplishments. I challenged him to see that being present with his employees and his family is the biggest accomplishment he can achieve. As technology moves at such a fast pace, many of us get caught up feeling the need to be at peak performance. At times this can feel easier than taking time to be present for ourselves and our loved ones. Meditation helps you slow down and be present.

I am not telling you that sitting quietly and breathing is easy. Actually, it can be difficult. You may have so many thoughts running through your mind it is hard to concentrate. When I started meditation, my mind was the master thought producer. I fidgeted a lot. My body was uncomfortable with being still. I felt like I had to move.

This is perfectly okay. As you focus on your breathing, even if you have a lot of thoughts and emotions initially, you will be achieving a greater level of mental clarity once your meditation time is complete. My meditation time sometimes contains a lot of thoughts, but I have noticed when I meditate before bed, even with all the thoughts, I am still able to sleep better. This tells me meditation works.

Meditation can be a metaphor for life. If you are frustrated or making judgments about your ability to be at peace during meditation, it is possible you are judging yourself too harshly in other areas of your life as well. My recommendation is to simply surrender and let go. There is nothing to do during meditation, only someone to be. Breathe, let go of judgment as you practice meditation. My beloved Bikram yoga teacher said, "Being still and calming the mind is the most difficult aspect of a yoga practice with postures."

There are two forms of meditation that provide deep healing: the simple seated breathing meditation and the guided meditation. Some people prefer guided meditation when they are starting out as it allows you to follow along and it guides you. However, at some point, I encourage you to do the simple breathing meditation. I also want to encourage you to meditate with others. When I meditate with others, I more easily achieve the sweet spot, which is similar to the runner's high sensation, and I go deeper into meditation quicker. I am not exactly sure how it works, but it works.

As you meditate, your body is so intelligent and it takes this quiet time to heal. Meditation is one of the best gifts you can give yourself on this journey and for life.

COACHING ACTION

1. Set your alarm for five, ten, or fifteen minutes.
2. Sit with a straight spine. Take three deep breaths in and out. Relax. Close your eyes.

3. Feel the connection of your legs to the chair or your back to the chair or wherever you are seated. Feel solidly connected to wherever you are.

4. Follow your breath in and out. Focus on your breathing.

5. If you want to, say a simple word as you breathe in.

6. If you have thoughts, allow them to float away and simply come back to your breath.

7. Sit quietly and focus on connecting deeply to your inner core.

8. Continue to breathe and feel yourself relax deeper.

9. Once you are complete, take a few moments, and notice how different you feel.

If you would prefer a guided meditation practice, I have included one in the appendix of this book (See Appendix A: Simple Guided Meditation Practice for Accessing Your Divine Love and Embracing a Natural High).

Natural Healing Method 6: Darkness, Pain, and the Black Rabbit Hole

From darkness, there is light.

Full disclosure, I have felt depressed at times on this journey and in life. I have been on my knees more than once, down in that dark hole of pain. Trying to figure out how to love myself was so hard at times. I believed I was such a failure on so many occasions. On a few of these occasions, I went down into the black rabbit hole, as I call it, of pain. Each time, I scaled the walls, clawing and screaming, to get out of that hole I had spiraled down into. Only because I have experienced this process can I understand the healing benefit it can provide.

Something very important was revealed to me during this journey into and back out of the black hole. The truth is sometimes you have to get all the way into the darkness to find the light within yourself. This black hole is filled with old emotions and feelings which have usually been buried for a very long time in your subconscious. These subconscious emotions linger from one point in our lives when we felt we would not survive or believed we were not worthy of surviving. Usually, these old subconscious feelings and thoughts are triggered by an event in our life such as the ending of a relationship. This triggering event brings up all our old fears and emotions. We are re-experiencing them as an adult in order to heal ourselves.

Being able to feel these deep feelings and emotions you sometimes had no idea existed, unlocks them from deep within your soul. Once we experience them, surrender to them, and come out of this place of darkness, we gain confidence in ourselves that we can survive this pain. We now know we can take care of ourselves.

Going through this brings you to a new level of life and freedom. You now have a compassion and knowledge for yourself you did not have before. Allowing yourself to go into the darkness is an opportunity to know yourself deeper.

If you are currently going through a time of darkness, know you are loved and safe. My advice is to allow yourself the time to cry and grieve, let the old junk out, and just be with the emotion, feel the emotion. And a very tough love message from me and my heart: *If you ever feel like you are not going to be safe with yourself, you must reach out for support.*

As I finish this book, those days thankfully seem so long ago. However, many of my journal entries are filled with this deep pain and the process I went through to heal it. This is important for me to share with you because I want you to know my life has not always looked like it looks now. Many of those dark days appeared once I started this path of self-love and moved to Colorado. I did not have any full-time work and had completely uprooted myself. This gave me a lot of time to process, which I really resisted. I am so grateful for that time now. I believe I could never know the happiness I have now if I had not gone through the darkness. Those dark days are a memory at this point and I attribute that to all the natural healing I have done.

SHARING MY STORY
Going into the Black Hole after Moving to Boulder, Colorado

Freedom—January 14, 2007

On this national holiday, Martin Luther King, Jr. Day, I am reminded of this great man's message of freedom that has always touched my soul. Recently, I have been fighting for my own personal freedom. The past few months were some of the most challenging of my life. I ended a relationship and recently moved to a new location, a thousand miles from where I had always called home. I have minimal income coming in, not even enough to pay my bills. However, it has been during this time of deep suffering that I have used my own strength to allow me to know and realize a deep freedom within.

One of the major keys to our freedom is understanding we must choose it for ourselves and, at times, we must fight for it. These past few months there were times when I felt like I did not want to live. This is a difficult thing for me to share. After failing once again in a relationship, I went to the depths of my personal sorrow. This was an unparalleled darkness for me. I had never allowed myself to go to this place. I always had previously been too busy. I wished I could stuff it all down and go to a job. I had no job, just building my business in Boulder, Colorado. I wanted to work, so I could forget the pain, but it had other ideas. It wanted to surface so I could heal it. My pain was not about the guy who left me; it was about my old issues related to abandonment and attachment. During this time of deep suffering, I feared it would never stop.

I stayed with it, embraced it even though it was extremely hard, and it did finally subside, but it took me to the depths of my soul. I could hardly eat and each day felt like a struggle to be alive. I had a good friend who took care of me during this time and it was a true gift. I made it through and you can, too.

At the point I went through this challenging time in 2007, I had not yet understood the importance of connecting to the Divine Mother within us. I share this next healing method here, as it may be an easier way through this pain. If you have already gone through your pain, you can still use this method to take care of you and be your own best mother.

Natural Healing Method 7: Connecting to the Divine Mother

Many individuals in this world may not have felt nurtured as children. Even if you did have adequate nurturing as a child, somehow the ability to provide this for yourself as an adult may have become forgotten. It is your birthright to find and cultivate this nurturing from within as an adult. You must reconnect with and nurture yourself in order to be able to love yourself fully. When you nurture yourself and take the time to connect to what I call the divine mother within, you are able to know at a deep level you are taken care of and are safe in everything you do. Connecting back to this part of yourself is very healing and calming. Male or female, we can all benefit from this meditation. Connecting to this mother energy within allows you to develop trust in yourself.

Mother

We are all mothers of our own souls
Our soul longs for nurture

It wonders why we focus outward,
Always expecting love from somewhere else
As it lies sad and alone

You are your own mother, dear one
When you truly understand this, you will be free

You and only you
Know the needs you have deep within

Take time, be calm, and listen
Your heart will speak, it will open up to you

Allow yourself this gift,
This gift of loving yourself

You will bring your peace into the world
A world that awaits your love

~ Shannon R. Rios

COACHING ACTION

1. Take a deep breath.
2. Close your eyes.
3. Relax your body by breathing deep.
4. Envision a beautiful place you have been to or seen. It is safe and peaceful.
5. See a woman about fifty feet from you standing in this place. She exudes a loving, safe, feminine, mother energy. You can see the divine energy surround her. You feel this, and it feels so safe. She is the perfect, loving mother. You can envision Mother Mary energy or any other very loving mother you have heard of or experienced in your life.
6. Walk toward this angelic woman. You can feel her strong and loving presence. She is holding her arms wide open to you. Connect with her and feel yourself receiving a huge heart-filled loving hug from her. Take this love in. Feel it now in your body; she is giving love to you. Breathe into this love. Accept this love. Receive this love.
7. As she hugs you, feel her energy completely merge with your energy. Feel this deep motherly love in your body. This is who you are. Breathe into this peace-filled energy.

8. Allow this safe love to fill your entire body. You may even feel as if you are floating, as your body shifts with this new energy flowing through it. Breathe into this.

9. Know you always have access to this infinite love and energy at any time. You are this pure love.

10. Close your eyes and breathe in this loving feminine mother energy for at least the next minute.

Natural Healing Method 8: Movement

In her book, *Molecules of Emotion*, author Candice Pert writes that it has been scientifically documented that we store emotions in the cells of our bodies. We physically hold old emotions and pain. Once you understand this, it makes sense that you would want to learn how to release these old emotions. They create the stories you still embrace about your past that can deeply affect you and play out through your life. If you can find ways to allow yourself to release old memories or beliefs, you can find new pathways into the world; allowing your blocked rivers to flow.

You may have read books or talked to someone in order to help yourself heal in the past. Intelligence, knowledge, and understanding can only take you so far. To release old patterns, you must bring the body and spirit into the process.

Your body learns and heals through movement or even the lack of it, in the case of meditation or other energy healing methods. In my life-coaching practice, I have made it mandatory that individuals agree to take on a body practice when they begin coaching with me. I recommend body-centered practices like dancing, yoga, walking, or meditation. If people want the optimum result in their lives, the body plays a significant role.

COACHING ACTION

1. What movement do you know you need to incorporate into your life (e.g., dance, jogging, kickboxing, tai chi, meditation, yoga)?
2. Sit for a few moments and ask yourself:
   What movement is crucial for me to begin doing in my life?
   What movement does my body need to be healthy?
   When will I begin?

Simple Movement Coaching

This is a great practice to do every morning or at any point during your day.

1. Stand up and just gently begin to move your body. Your body will tell you how it wants to move and stretch. You could also put on some soothing music.
2. Close your eyes and take ten deep breaths. As you breathe deeply, move and stretch your body any way it wants.
3. Sit back down, take a couple deep breaths, and feel the difference in your body. What do you notice?

Natural Healing Method 9: A Healthy Spine and Back

Over time, emotions can become stuck in your body and manifest as physical pain. While writing my last revision of this book, I struggled with tremendous lower back pain. It was so painful it was a challenge for me to sit and write. Through my research, I learned back pain is a very common phenomenon in society today. I believe it comes from two things: our past histories/traumas and our current work environments. We still need to work, so what can we do?

I took time, sat and meditated, and asked what I needed to do for this chronic back pain. What my intuition told me is I needed to do the following practice with my body. It is important I share this method with you due to the overwhelming amount of people who struggle with back and neck pain. All yogis know a healthy spine and back are crucial for our overall health.

COACHING ACTION

1. Sit upright on the floor, sofa, or any flat surface with your spine straight and your legs crossed or feet flat on the floor. Do not curve your spine. Tighten your stomach or core so your lower back actually tucks under a bit.

2. Take a deep breath. Feel and connect to your sex organs and elimination organs. No matter where you're sitting, envision the base of your spine touching and connecting with the ground or chair.

3. Begin to tighten your muscles softly in this area, sometimes called the pelvic floor. If you are familiar with yoga, you will know this motion as Mul Bandh. You can also think of stopping the flow of urine from your body and that will give you the sensation that's intended.

4. Envision you have a bowl. The bowl's base is the bottom of your perineum or sex organ area, resting on the ground or chair just as your bottom does. The sides of the bowl come up into your sex organs. The bowl is holding your sex organs. Now, move the area of your body around in a circle, like you are Latin dancing, moving these lower chakras or energy centers. Move the area slowly. Breathe. Pretend you have water in the bowl and you are sloshing it around but it is not spilling over because you are slow and deliberate. Take a deep breath.

5. Focus on moving any energy in this area that feels stuck or blocked. You are moving from your bottom up to navel level. If you have any pain in this area, ask your body what this pain is. Listen for the answer.

6. Now, begin to feel this energy start to uncoil and slowly make its way up your spine, one vertebra at a time. If you were looking down at your spine, this energy is moving clockwise up your spine. You are slowly moving your body as you move the energy up your spine. Close your eyes and take a deep breath. Envision this beautiful energy moving up your spine slowly, winding through and around your spine. Envision this motion moving your spinal fluid. Breathe deep.

7. Continue feeling this uncoiling energy moving all the way up to the top of your neck.

8. Begin to move your spine in the opposite direction. Bring the energy back down your spine in the opposite direction, still winding it around your spine.

9. When you are back at the bottom, once again move the center of your hip area in the round motion, envisioning the water you have in your bowl. Move it now counter-clockwise or the opposite direction you moved it before.

10. Feel the energy again moving up your spine. Stop anywhere you feel pain. Focus on this spot on your spine. Breathe into the pain. When you get to the top of your spine and neck, move all the way back down to your bottom and to the ground or floor. Move your water around in your bowl in whatever way feels good to your body.

11. Visualize this beautiful channel you have created in your spine. Breathe deeply into this new energy you have opened up in your body.

This exercise is very powerful because our bodies are healthy when our spines are healthy. When we envision moving our spinal fluid, we create positive benefits to our spine. Your lower back and spine are crucial aspects of your movement, health, and creativity.

Get up from your chair periodically during the day and do this exercise standing. You can also do it sitting. It will provide many benefits including getting your creativity flowing again. I sometimes do this lower body movement when driving the car. Getting this energy moving is instrumental to your physical and mental health.

Practice this movement whenever you can. Now a daily part of my morning meditation, this exercise has helped me transform and heal my lower back pain.

Natural Healing Method 10: Mothering Yourself

I end with this healing method because at this point in your self-love journey you must deeply understand you are your best mother. You must now take care of yourself, your inner child, and not expect anyone else to do it. When you desperately want others to take care of you, it usually originates from an old wounded part of yourself. It is the small child inside crying for *you* to pay attention to them. No one else can take care of you the way you can.

Years ago in the midst of my sadness and depression, I took the time to connect with myself to listen to my inner child. In times of deep upset or stress, it really is the small child inside who is inconsolable. On one day of my deepest depression, I got a hold of myself and took the time to mother me. When I asked her what she needed, my inner child advised me to eat protein. I cooked myself an egg and felt much better. I needed to mother myself by eating well. This is not something that always came easily to me. Taking time to mother yourself and your child inside allows you to find out what you truly need.

COACHING ACTION

This exercise allows you to mother yourself by connecting to your child within. This exercise is good if you are in deep pain or feel overwhelmed. It can be done even if you are not in pain. Use it whenever you want to simply connect more deeply with your inner child and find out what she needs.

1. Take a deep breath.
2. Relax your body, let any tension go.
3. Envision now you are holding a baby in your arms. Actually hold your arms like you are holding a baby. This baby is you.
4. Feel the love you have for this magnificent child. Close your eyes and breathe deeply into this love.
5. Say to this child, *Beautiful child, I am always here with you; I can never leave you. You are safe here with me. I love you.* Say anything else your child needs to hear.
6. Look at this angelic, vulnerable child like you would any other baby. Feel that love. Breathe deeply into this love.
7. Rock the child gently, or find a rocker and rock her. Rocking is good for balancing and calming your brain.
8. Ask, *What do you need from me?* Listen to the response; your inner child will let you know.
9. Ask any other questions you would like to ask.
10. Do this exercise for the next ten days, or whenever you feel upset and need to connect with this child. Get to know your inner child; her wisdom will empower you.

Summary

All of these natural methods can assist you in cultivating deep self-love. Know you also have the ability to create your own healing processes in the moment when you need them. Always remember, you are your own best healer.

ALLOW DIVINE PEACE WITHIN

During my thirteen-year quest for self-love, I have come to understand achieving peace within is the closest you will ever get to complete happiness and satisfaction in life. It is not about anything or anyone. True peace is about releasing any attachment to what you *should* be, what you *should* do, or what you *should* have in life. You know you are in the right place because *you are you and because you were chosen to be born.*

Take a deep breath and take it in. You trust this is your perfect path because you know you are here to develop this greater peace inside. It is not perfect in the sense that all is correct. It is perfect because you know you are here for a reason. You trust things are in divine order and are working themselves out. You choose this path consciously, you forgive, you accept what appears, and you receive with an open heart. You make the choice to live your life on purpose, no matter how crazy you may feel some days. You make the choice each moment to accept and embrace your life.

Peace within is knowing you are pure love. It means knowing you are here to share your unique gifts and love in the world.

Peace is a sense of inner contentment and having enough abundance to live in this world freely. It is the freedom to do what you want and contribute the way you want in the world. It is expressing your gifts in the world. True peace is a process of knowing what is right for *you*, for your soul, in this lifetime.

Inner peace comes from opening and following your heart, from being present wherever you are. Today, as I write, I am listening to the quiet gurgle of the creek flowing by me in a graceful, beautiful way. As I sit here meditating, the wind speaks to me. It blows the aspen leaves over me, floating down like love notes, speaking deeply to my soul. They are telling me of all the love in the world.

As I continue to meditate, one of the leaves becomes caught in my hair, a gentle reminder that I am never alone. My body shivers with the knowledge of being loved and nurtured by nature, and I realize I am always surrounded by the love of the Universe. I reach up and gently touch this leaf that has found a home in my hair, I feel its soft texture. Feeling this deep connection to nature and how it nurtures me, tears well up. The message I hear for all of us, no matter what our current situation, is:

You are pure. You are whole. You are love.

When we realize this, we are at peace. Yes, once we reach this place, something will inevitably interrupt this contentment, but the important thing is to know deep down this feeling can be achieved again and again and again. Once you know it exists, you can return anytime. Be aware of this fact, and whenever you leave this space of serenity, know you intend to be back. It is that simple. The more you practice returning to this place of awareness, the easier it will become.

SHARING MY STORY
Living in the Flow and Changing My Name

On July 12, 2006, at the age of thirty-five, I officially changed my last name to Rios. It was something I knew I needed to do to fully embrace myself and this journey I was on.

I loved the name Shannon Rivers and since I love the Spanish language, I decided to become Shannon Rios.

I knew deep inside I wanted to take a new name. It felt as though it was time for me to have my own name. We sometimes change our names when we marry someone. Why not change it when we commit to ourselves? I was ready. This was a big juncture in my life. I was moving to Colorado and publishing my first book soon. I wanted to give myself my own name, one that was meaningful to me. My intent with my new name was peaceful, flowing rivers. My previous name was Bonkrude, i.e., *bonk* and *rude*. It had never felt like it fit my spirit once I started my self-love journey. I was determined with my move to take my life in a new direction.

When you do something like this, you create some waves. Once I made this change, I actually had quite a few rapids to go through before I arrived at my peaceful flowing life, my river. There were ebbs and flows, to be sure. I also had many strange reactions from friends and family. The most interesting was a friend who called me, angry I had not told her I had gotten married. The other interesting occurrence was when someone I chose not to work with said to me, "Well, obviously you are an unhappy, divorced woman." Since I did not look like a Rios, he incorrectly assumed I was divorced. Those who knew me well were happy for this next chapter in my life.

I did not get what the fuss was about. My mind says we should be able to change our name when *we* choose. We should be free to take someone else's name, keep our given name, or change our name on our own. It just seems normal to me. This decision really propelled me onto my own path. I do follow the road less traveled. The truth is, to me, it seems like the only road.

I share this story because I want you to always listen to yourself and do what is right for you. I want you to know you can stand up to mainstream thoughts whenever you want.

Peace Within—Lesson 1: The Wise Woman

As I finished this book, twelve years after I began it, the memory of a very wise woman came into my mind. Her message belongs here in the last chapter. As we continue to love ourselves, we must continue to practice embracing our beauty and love.

I met a very wise woman on a plane a few years ago. Her story was she had adopted twelve children, and her adopted children had come with some horrific stories and backgrounds. The agency would call her when they had an extra special child and situation. When she told me of the successes of her children, now adults, I could hardly believe what I heard. They were married, attended college, had their own children, and lived successful lives. This was not the expected outcome for children who had come from such dire early circumstances. I turned in my seat and looked deep into her eyes and asked her, because I knew the miracle she had accomplished, "What did you do?" She told me two things:

> *"I told them that before they got to me, God and the angels had been with them every minute, taking care of them, loving them, and leading them to me. They never felt they were alone.*
>
> *I looked deep in their eyes with complete love every single time I looked at them. I saw myself as their mirror of love every single time they looked at me, the love they had not known before from others. I saw them as complete love and nothing else."*

This wisdom is beautiful and brilliant. She promised these children they were always cared for. She gave them the security inside of knowing they were always loved. She then filled them with deep and unconditional love every time she looked at them. That continuous love healed the deep attachment wounds of these children and allowed them to live into their full potential of love expressed in the world. They knew at their core they were safe, valuable, and loved.

COACHING ACTION

As we are nearing the end of this journey together, please allow me the honor of being your wise woman.

First, I want to tell you: *Before you came to me and the lessons of this book, the angels were with you every minute, taking care of you. You have always been loved and cared for.* Breathe into this truth.

Second, I want you to imagine me looking at you with pure, deep love in my eyes because I am. Look up from the page and see me here with you. Imagine I see all of your beauty inside. I am reflecting the pure love inside of you back to you right now with tears in my eyes. Feel this love. Breathe into my love. I say to you now, *you are pure love; I see your brilliance.* See me saying this to you. Receive this in, accept you are deeply loved, and breathe deep into this truth. See and hear me saying this to you seven more times: *You are pure love; I see your brilliance.*

Peace Within—Lesson 2: Reflect Your Own Love

The other crucial teaching I want to leave you with allows you to reflect love, beauty, and peace to yourself. When you can do this for yourself, you can get through anything. It calms worry, fear, and anxiety because you deeply know you are always there for you.

I have adapted this exercise, so you can do this with your child inside. This exercise has the ability to shift you at a deep level, just as the woman on the plane shifted her children. It is a wonderful exercise to complete with your partners and children.

COACHING ACTION

This Wise Woman Meditation was created in honor of the wise adoptive mother on the plane.

1. Take three deep breaths.
2. Relax your body.
3. Close your eyes.
4. In your mind's eye, imagine yourself as a baby.
5. Hold this baby, who is you, in your arms.

6. Look the baby, yourself as a child, directly in her eyes, as you tenderly hold her.

7. Feel the love from your core deep inside of yourself, and send this love to the baby. Gaze into this beautiful child's eyes, you as a baby, with complete love and adoration. See only the beauty. Breathe deep. Let her know everything is going to be okay; you are here with her. Any worries she has are going to be okay. Do this for as long as you can, breathing deeply. Feel yourself as a child relax, knowing you are safe and secure. Feel this circle of love going from you to the baby and back to you.

8. Now say to this precious child: *You are beautiful. You are brilliant. You can do anything. You are pure love. I am always here.* Look at this child with your pure unconditional love. Send this love to her. Let her know she is completely safe.

9. Now, feel this love returning back to you as your adult self. Feel yourself accept this love and integrate all of this love into yourself right now. Feel this beauty inside that you truly are.

10. Breathe this in.

11. Allow any emotion.

12. Close your eyes and feel this love.

Peace Within—Lesson 3: Connection to Your Own Inner Peace

When you are able to see your internal beauty, you can choose to see beauty in the world, deeply connect to it, and completely receive it. As you recognize and accept your inner peace, you can create peace in whatever circumstances you find yourself. Connecting to yourself is one of the most important gifts you give yourself in this life. There are so many distractions at this point in our history. You now have to focus on this even more, so you can recharge your battery and be the model for peace and connection in the world.

COACHING ACTION

To strengthen and continue this journey of love and peace, the following actions are important.

- Be thankful each day for the life you have.
- Remember you have a choice each day, each moment.
- Connect to nature and nurture you every chance you get.
- Breathe, laugh, and smile—each one changes your paradigm.
- Take time out to do something you enjoy each day—this is your life.
- Meditate and manifest peace each day—it will calm your mind.
- Plan solo trips just to be with *you*.
- Practice quiet time every day.

Peace Within—Lesson 4: Loving You Through Loving Thoughts

Loving you takes continuous practice. The healing process involved with loving yourself is one of discovery each day. As you heal, life opens up and becomes more beautiful, and as a result, you will become happier. I followed this path of self-love and now twelve years later as I finish this book I am married to a wonderful man and we are in the process of beginning our family together. Whatever your dream is, it will manifest if you choose this path.

One thing I know that has assisted me in being successful is positive affirmations and thoughts. Our thoughts create our reality. Our life is a mirror of our thoughts. To manifest your dreams you must ensure your thoughts are in alignment with the life you desire to have. This is a key to your transformation. The power of our mind is truly our greatest power. When you believe, you receive.

COACHING ACTION

The following affirmations are an integral part of realizing self-love and moving toward the contentment, satisfaction, and happiness you so richly deserve.

They are affirmations I used at different points in my journey to ensure I stayed on the path.

1. Read through the affirmations below.
2. After each one, take a deep breath and notice any emotional reactions. This emotional reaction lets you know these are important for you. For me, the important ones seem to have a charge when I read them.
3. Put an * by the ones you know are important to you.
4. Read the important ones every day.
5. Believe they are true now, even if they have not been true for you in the past.

> *I will always love you.*
> *I will always accept you.*
> *I will keep you safe.*
> *I will always be with you.*
> *I will always stay with you.*
> *I will always hold you, especially when you cry.*
> *I will rock you.*
> *I will nourish and feed you.*
> *I will tell you I love you.*
> *I will take care of you and your body.*
> *I will have fun with you.*
> *I will be patient with you.*
> *I will always speak kindly to you.*

I will be with people who show you they love you.
I will forever love you.

Peace Within—Lesson 5: YOU are the ONE

I must leave you with a last imperative message. No matter what your relationship status is, you are your forever one. No one completes you like you. Once you accept this, it takes so much pressure off your romantic relationships or lack of romantic relationships. Loving you is the one thing you can always do to be happy. Whether you are in a relationship or not, loving you will provide you the ability to create more successful relationships. Focus on you, not them.

SHARING MY STORY
The Big Realization So I Could Publish This Book

As I was completing this book, Jonas and I were discussing marriage. I loved him and in truth I had my doubts and fears, which was actually pretty normal for me. A year prior to this, when I was in a deep meditation with Yoga Nidra, I had asked if Jonas was the one for me and I heard a strong "no." This honestly stressed me out.

One evening I was taking a hot bath to take care of myself prior to Jonas's arrival from Sweden. We had discussed getting married during this trip. I asked again if he was the one for me. Again I heard a strong "no." I thought this was so frustrating and confusing. Was I making the wrong choice? Since commitment is hard for me, I became stressed wondering if I was making a wrong choice.

Therefore, I did what I knew I needed to do to listen to myself closely. I got really quiet and listened deeply for what this answer meant. I clearly heard... **you are the "one."** With tears in my eyes and a big sigh of relief, I laughed. This was one of my last lessons I had to understand before I could fully commit to Jonas and I could finally finish this book. I had to remember no one else could ever be the one for me, except me.

COACHING ACTION

What does it mean to you to be the one for you?
Are you clear that you are your one?
How will this help you in your relationships?
What do you need to do to practice being the one in your life?

Peace Within—Lesson 6: Integration into Your Life

Know you will now begin a huge process of integrating all you have read and the coaching actions you have completed. Reading this book is just the beginning. Everything you have completed has deepened your access to your own self-love. Embrace this truth.

The information you have processed will now unfold in your life. Your subconscious has taken in more than you realize. You will see the shifts begin to occur. You may feel strange at times; that is normal. You are reorganizing yourself and how you relate to the world. Change can feel messy and sometimes disruptive. If you feel this way, know you are on the right path. You will have highs and lows. That is all part of the beautiful process.

Breathe into it. Continue to return to your sacred space inside. There is nothing more to do, just focus on being you.

With everything you have learned in this book, you now have the skills to continue to heal and grow as you embrace your life. What you need to reach your next level of potential is always manifested when you ask for it. You are divinely protected and guided, this is truth. You have your own unique path. You and you alone are your best guide.

Caution, no matter what age you are, your entire life is now ahead of you.

~ Shannon Rios Paulsen

My best coaching at this point is to tell you to live life like you are on a trip where you don't know what really comes next, but you are excited for the moment when you see that next beautiful vista. Live in excitement, knowing you have the skills and the attitude to live your life fully with no regrets. That, my dear friend, is the very good news.

Allow, live each day, and let go like the beautiful flowing river of life. You are a seeker of life. Continue seeking. Have patience and enjoy the ride.

A woman in harmony with her spirit is like a river flowing. She goes where she will without pretense and arrives at her destination prepared to be herself and only herself.

~ Maya Angelou

In Love & Gratitude

I want to thank you from the depth of my heart for taking this journey with me. It has been my complete and humble honor to partner with you. I send each of you love and light every day. As I am finishing my book, my sweet furry companion, Sassy, passed in my arms after twelve years of partnership. It was the hardest thing I have ever been through as an adult and at the same time, it was a deep honor to be with her as her spirit left this physical world. You are entering this world on your journey, and the honor of ushering you in feels similar. Thank you so much. We are on this journey together forever. I am so grateful to call you part of my family here on Earth.

Know I hold you in my heart and I love you—truly, madly, deeply… and forever in infinity.

Until we meet again,

Shannon Rios Paulsen

As you continue...

YOUR JOURNEY

You are on a path of love. Take a deep breath and ask yourself, *Should I continue this journey with the support of the best self-love teachers and coaches?* If your answer is yes, I invite you to continue this journey in some way. I have many resources I recommend at the back of this book. I also have offerings for anyone who reads this book and wants to continue this journey of self-love. We hold tele-classes for the readers of this book to continue to support you in bringing your peace and love into the world.

Go to www.inlovewithme.com/bookspecials to sign up for ongoing support along your way. You can also take the post-book Love Quiz to see how you are doing after reading the book (found in Appendix B).

One final step...

COACHING ACTION

In answering the following questions, don't think too long, just ask yourself, and listen for the immediate answer.

What one next step do you want to take to continue this work of self-love in your life?
What do you want to honor or acknowledge yourself for in this moment?
What have you done that is really amazing already?
What are you grateful for?

Epilogue

As I finished one of the final rounds of editing this book, my beautiful daughter, Emma Emaya, was born into this world. With tears in my eyes, I tell you sincerely from my heart that I do not believe this would have been possible without me taking this journey of self-love seriously. I wanted a partner and a family and I knew self-love was the road to get me there.

I was right, and the journey always continues. She is my beautiful butterfly, allowing this caterpillar to grow its wings.

I love you all. Thank you for sharing this journey with me. I am forever grateful to all of you.

Appendix A

SIMPLE, GUIDED MEDITATION PRACTICE FOR ACCESSING YOUR DIVINE LOVE AND EMBRACING A NATURAL HIGH

I have witnessed many people seeking a high from substances. However, this borrowed high does not provide you the opportunity to heal and find your own true peace within. This meditation connects you to your divine soul, so you can find your natural high. You may want to have someone else read this to you or record this for yourself.

1. Sit comfortably. You can sit on a sofa if you like. It does not matter how you sit. I personally prefer to have my legs crossed, but this is not a requirement.
2. Take three deep breaths.
3. Envision a golden ball of magical colors spinning at the crown or top of your head. The ball is about the size of a tennis ball.
4. Visualize this ball dropping down through your head, neck, and chest at the midline of your body.
5. Stop the ball when it gets to your stomach or solar plexus chakra. This is your core. This is where you are very powerful. Breathe into this.
6. See the golden ball of many colors spinning there in the middle of your body. It is simply beautiful, just as you are.

7. Slow the ball down until it is spinning slowly and gently in slow motion.

8. Whenever you have a thought, return to the spinning ball.

9. Sink deeper into your body as you stay focused on the ball of colors, not thinking about it, just focusing your attention there.

10. If it helps you to focus, you may also think of one word "OM" in your mind while focusing on the ball.

11. When it feels right, take another deep breath. Allow your breathing to move into its natural state.

12. The goal is to focus on the ball, go deep inside yourself, and release all other thoughts. At some point, you may no longer see the ball, and this is fine.

13. With each exhale, allow your body to relax and release. Feel yourself sinking deeper into your center. It is an angelic feeling when you access this place of peace and divine love inside yourself.

14. We all have this peaceful place within. We can all access it; it just may take some practice.

15. After two to five minutes, envision the sphere getting bigger and bigger until the ball of color and power encircles your body. This is your true internal power. Surround yourself with this infinite power. What does this power hold for you? Peace? Calm? Love? Breathe into this. You can now move into the world in this power, moving from your beautiful center.

Post Love Quiz

Scale of 1-10 (1 = strongly disagree; 10 = strongly agree)

I believe I can heal myself.	1 2 3 4 5 6 7 8 9 10
I feel love for myself.	1 2 3 4 5 6 7 8 9 10
I know I have a divine purpose in this lifetime.	1 2 3 4 5 6 7 8 9 10
My relationships are healthy.	1 2 3 4 5 6 7 8 9 10
I can access a feeling of peace within.	1 2 3 4 5 6 7 8 9 10
I feel supported in life.	1 2 3 4 5 6 7 8 9 10
I have a healthy level of self-love.	1 2 3 4 5 6 7 8 9 10
I have skills to be able to return to my inner peace.	1 2 3 4 5 6 7 8 9 10

To Continue Your Journey
with Shannon

Thank you for taking time to read this book. As we all know, self-love is a journey and it will continue. I ask you to look into your heart and see what your next step will be. If you know there is a specific area you want to focus on, set that intention. The resources you need will show up, I firmly believe this. Open your heart to receive.

As a gift to you and to help you take this next step, we have created some special offers for those of you who have read this book. Practicing key concepts is crucial, as it will ensure they are imprinted into your consciousness.

Strength can come from accepting support from others. I am sending you love on this journey each and every day. Some days can be harder than others, know you are loved and supported. Please accept the support of some of the following resources.

<u>Self-Love Resources</u>

FREE —Heart-Opening Guided Meditation:
Shannon lovingly guides you to listen to messages of your heart.
<u>http://inlovewithme.com/heart-opening-meditation-free-gift</u>

FREE—Receiving Questionnaire:
Download the Receiving questionnaire to assess how well you receive and learn to receive more in your life.
<u>http://inlovewithme.com</u>

Life Coaching Sessions:
Take your life to the next level! Working one-on-one with Shannon is a priceless gift to yourself. Use coupon code **lifedeal** to receive a 25% discount on life coaching sessions.
http://inlovewithme.com/life-coaching

Guided Meditations:
The Healing Journey Within: Meditations for Abundance and Love: Volume I (Deserving) & Volume II (Manifesting)
by Shannon Rios MS LMFT
Give yourself this gift of deepening your self-love.
2 for 1: Download one and get the other free.
http://inlovewithme.com/two-for-one
OR
Amazon (hard copy or download):
Volume I: http://bit.ly/selflovemedvol1
Volume II: http://bit.ly/selflovemedvol2

Self-Love Book:
In Love With Me: Ten Steps to Self-Love and Successful Relationships by Shannon R Rios Paulsen, MS, LMFT.
Download is 50% off the cover price.
http://bit.ly/loveme7
OR
Amazon (hard copy or download): http://bit.ly/10stepsselflovebook

Motherhood & Fertility Coaching/Book:
Shannon coaches women whose dream is to become mothers later in life. Her book on fertility and motherhood is:
Manifesting Baby: The Mother's 30 Day Fertility Journal
www.manifestingbaby.com
http://inlovewithme.com/life-coaching

Parenting and Divorce Resources

Work one on one with Shannon and learn how to be the best parent and co-parent possible. A true gift to yourself and your children. Use coupon code **lifedeal** to receive a 25% discount on life coaching sessions.

http://inlovewithme.com/life-coaching

Parenting and Divorce Books:
The 7 Fatal Mistakes Divorced and Separated Parents Make: Strategies for Raising Healthy Children of Divorce and Conflict
Shannon's best-selling parenting and divorce book, give your kids this gift. Use coupon code **bookdeal** to receive 50% discount.

http://inlovewithme.com/books

OR

Amazon: http://bit.ly/divorceparentbook

Healthy Children of Divorce in 10 Simple Steps: Minimize the Effects of Divorce on Your Children
Shannon's second book on divorce and parenting, this comprehensive workbook provides you 10 simple steps to raise healthy children of divorce.

Amazon: http://bit.ly/10stepsdivorceparentbook

Parenting and Divorce Class on Video:
Shannon teaches her highly acclaimed class on children and divorce to provide you the secrets of raising healthy children of divorce. Discounted 50% to $29.99. Use coupon code **happykid** to receive discount.

http://bit.ly/divclass

Recommended Reading

Melody Beattie, *Beyond Codependency: And Getting Better All the Time.* Center City, MN: Hazelden, 1989.

Melody Beattie, *Codependent No More.* Center City, MN: Hazelden: 1986.

Leo F. Buscaglia, *Loving Each Other: The Challenge of Human Relationships.* New York, NY: Ballantine Books, 1986.

John Bradshaw, *Healing the Shame that Binds You.* Revised Ed. Deerfield Beach, FL: HCI, 2005.

Gary D. Chapman, *The 5 Love Languages: The Secret to Love that Lasts.* New Ed. Chicago, IL: Northfield Publishing, 2010.

Deepak Chopra, *The Path to Love.* New York, NY: Random House, 1998.

Deepak Chopra, *Ageless Body, Timeless Mind: The Quantum Alternative to Growing Old.* New York, NY. Random House, 1993, 1998, 2010.

Sonia Choquette, *Your Heart's Desire: Instructions for Creating the Life You Really Want.* New York, NY: Potter Style, 1997.

David Deida, *Dear Lover: A Woman's Guide to Men, Sex, and Love's Deepest Bliss.* Louisville, CO: Sounds True, 2005.

Anne Frank, *The Diary of a Young Girl.* Edited by Otto Frank and Mirjam Pressler. Reprint. New York, NY: Random House, 1993.

Viktor E. Frankl, *Man's Search for Meaning.* Boston, MA: Beacon Press, 2006.

Thich Nhat Hanh, True Love: *A Practice for Awakening the Heart.* First American Ed. Boston, MA: Shambhala, 2006.

Thom Hartmann, *Walking Your Blues Away: How to Heal the Mind and Create Emotional Well-Being*. Rochester, VT: Park Street Press, 2010.

Harville Hendrix, *Getting the Love You Want: A Guide for Couples*. 20th An. Ed. New York, NY: St. Martin's Press, 2008.

Susan Jeffers, *Feel the Fear and Do It Anyway*. 20th An. Ed. New York, NY: Ballantine Books, 2006.

Jon Kabat-Zinn, *Wherever You Go, There You Are: Mindfulness Meditation in Everyday Life*. 10th Ed. New York, NY: Hyperion: 2005.

Charlotte Kasl, *If the Buddha Dated: A Handbook for Finding Love on a Spiritual Path*. New York, NY: Penguin, 1999.

Amir Levine, *Attached: The New Science of Adult Attachment and How It Can Help You Find—and Keep—Love*. Reprint Ed. New York, NY: Tarcher, 2012.

Candace Pert, *Molecules of Emotion: Why You Feel the Way You Feel*. Scribner. New York, NY. 1997.

Eva Pierrakos, *Creating Union: The Essence of Intimate Relationship*. Edited by Judith Saly. 2nd edition. Madison, VA: Pathwork Press, 2002.

Shannon R. Rios, *The 7 Fatal Mistakes Divorced and Separated Parents Make: Strategies for Raising Healthy Children of Divorce and Conflict*. LifeThreads Books: Evergreen, CO: 2009.

Mattie J. T. Stepanek, *Reflections of a Peacemaker: A Portrait through Heartsongs*. Andrews McNeel Publishing: 2005.

Shefali Tsabary, *The Conscious Parent*. Vancouver, Canada: Namaste Publishing, 2010.

Andrew T. Weil, Health and Healing: *The Philosophy of Integrative Medicine and Optimum Health*. Rev. Ed. New York, NY: Mariner Books, 2004.

John Welwood, *Perfect Love, Imperfect Relationships: Healing the Wound of the Heart*. Westville, South Africa: Trumpeter, 2007.